To Gary & J

" Next year in Jerusalem

" לשנה הבאה עיר ושלים "

Blessings,

shakked

July 2022

x'

SECRET ISRAEL

SECRET ISRAEL

The Israel Most Visitors Miss

SHAKKED BEERY

2021

Editor: Sam Sachs
Illustrations: Dillon Krueger

ISBN: 978-965-599-668-5

SECRET ISRAEL

לאבא

נמרוד בארי 1959-2013
איש עבודה ורוח, מלח הארץ, שלימד אותי הרפתקה, תעוזה,
אהבת הארץ ואהבת אדם.

לסבא

יחיאל בארי 1927-2001
איש פלמ"ח ומורה דרך בישראל שבעקבותיו הלכתי
ובעבור ספר הטיולים בגולן שכתב, אך מעולם לא זכה להוציא לאור.

For Dad (Le Aba)

Nimrod Be'ery 1959-2013
A man of labor and spirit, salt of the earth, who taught me
adventure, audacity and the love of the land and its people.

For Grandpa (Le Saba)

Yechiel Be'ery 1927-2001
A Palmach warrior and tour guide in Israel,
whose footsteps I followed, and for the Golan travel guide
he wrote, but never got to publish.

CONTENTS

Preface

Welcome to Secret Israel – The Israel Most Visitors Miss.

What makes the content of this book a secret is that it gives you the Israel you can't get anywhere else.

If you're reading the preface to this book, it is almost a given that you find Israel interesting. Maybe you're dreaming about visiting it one day. Maybe you've visited it once and can't wait to go back. Maybe you've been there dozens of times and you're looking for things you haven't seen yet. Either way, something about Israel captured your heart, and if that's true – you and I have a lot in common.

Since 2011, my mission is to lead and support people through their journey in Israel. The biggest challenge about it has always been the abundance it has to offer as opposed to limitations of time or money. I always see visitors going on the plane back home, somewhat reluctantly. No matter how long the trip was, they always want to stay for a little bit longer.

Given that my mission was always to give people as much of Israel as they can possibly handle, it made me sad to see them returning to their homes. Both them and I know perfectly well that the journey isn't close to an end. Israel is an endless journey into our identity. The stories of it, are the stories of us. That's what makes it so attractive.

A warning to the traditional reader. This book is not like any book you've ever read. It is unique, as it brings the Israel that only I can bring you. I am not a university professor or a journalist. I am a tour guide in Israel. This means I bring the unique combination of intellect and storytelling. It means I learned how to collect the interesting bits of history that connect to our own lives, along with the fun and juicy details that are fun to read – and wove them into a collection of stories you can't read about anywhere else.

While all the historical details are backed with research and cited through the book for the reader's convenience, I do want to make one thing clear. This isn't so much of a book, as it is a trip.

Anyone who ever traveled anywhere knows that a good trip, one that stays with you years after its done, is a combination of exploration, fun and the human experience. This book was written not to add another book about Israel to the pile, but to present Israel like no one has before. Because this is my first book, I have no way of knowing yet whether I'm a good author or not. I do know, however, that I'm a fairly good tour guide, and my secret is my desire to see you get excited about Israel, so much so that you'll have a piece of it in your heart forever.

This book wasn't written to be a good book. It was written to be the trip I never got to guide, to the places in Israel I, the local Israeli Jew, love the most. It is an open invitation to enjoy Israel in the exact way that I enjoy it. I invite you to dive into the deep waters of knowledge and find where it connects to our lives today. I also invite you to immerse yourself into the human stories of the people who lived in this land and made it into the wonder that it is today.

If you visited the collection of places brought in this book in person, they will be remembered as the highlights of your trip, just because of how rare and untraveled they are. While a regular tour limits where we want to go and how long we get to spend there, "Secret Israel" allows us to travel to the hidden gems of Israel and spend as much time there as we want.

Much like a tour that would offer some history, some human encounters and some personal interactions with your guide, this book is also an eclectic experience. Some sections are historical and take an in-depth dive into research. Other sections will be fictionalized history and provide a unique point of view on historical events through the eyes of the characters that lived them. Between those two, Secret Israel is providing you with my personal experience of living in my country as an Israeli-Jewess.

Reading this book is an eye-level experience, told in a unique voice: Sometimes intellectual, sometimes storytelling, sometimes pondering, and sometimes humorous. It is as much as possible, a taste of the multi-flavored experience that is a good trip in Israel.

When traveling, different people enjoy different things. To make sure that this read is a fun experience for a variety of people, it is constructed so that if you don't like one of the destinations, or find one of the segments boring, you can jump right ahead to the next one, and your reading experience will stay the same.

Along with being a tour-guide, my other hat is an Israel Studies scholar. This isn't said in order to blow my own whistle, but in order to help guarantee that the research work put into this book is extensive, professional and valid. A lot of research was put into every site, with the strong desire of bringing you not just stories and a personal experience, but narratives anchored in scripture, archeological finds and up-to-date research. Each site in this book was chosen carefully, to make sure it has an interesting story that will survive the test of time and will continue being relevant for decades after reading this book.

My secret desire is to be able to bring my Israel, the one I love but never get to share, to the house of every person that already has Israel in their heart. I am thrilled by the thought of giving a voice to the hidden stories of my land. I pray that these stories will land on loving and knowledge-thirsty ears.

Israel is not just a place. It is an idea and a symbol. That's why so many people have so many opinions and feelings about it, but hardly anyone is indifferent to it. The importance of it cannot be underestimated. For this reason, it's often easy to get lost in the big news and lofty ideas, and lose the human aspect of it. From Biblical stories, to its fascinating history, and all the way into the personal experiences of living in Israel today, this book immerses you in the complex and nuanced place that is the Holy Land.

Wrapped within the publishing of this book is great excitement. Knowing that my Israel will leave the realm of personal storytelling and enter the public eye is both scary and thrilling. Since this book is a trip, if you chose to read it, you are my visitors, and this means I see myself as responsible for your Israel experience, from start to finish. Therefore, you can see it as an open invitation to always reach out to me and engage about everything Israel. I can't wait for you to join me in exploring Israel, Shakked's style. Now let's get this show on the road!

SECRET ISRAEL

Introduction:
The Things I Never Get to Do

Here they come, dragging their luggage behind them, looking both tired and excited. After 20 hours of flight, I am not surprised. They all have the same color lanyard around their necks and they're following the group's leader, his eyes searching for the sign with his name on it. I smile to myself when I see how he is trying to look energetic and excited, even though he must be even more exhausted than everyone else. Leading a group is a very demanding job, yet, from the point of view of the tourist, the group leader or the tour guide, are never tired. Thank God for Adrenalin.

As a matter of fact, even without 20 hours of flight and 50 people depending on my leadership skills, I was tired, having arrived at the airport at 4:30 in the morning. It's the kind of tiredness that even the ridiculously high-priced airport coffee can't cure. It always costs twice as much and tastes twice as bad. I often wonder if what woke me up was the double-shot espresso or the shock I got when I went to the register and heard how much it costs.

I held the sign higher up in the air and waved. The group-leader spotted me and an expression of "mission accomplished" appeared on his face. He quickly moved towards me, as if he'd caught a second wind. The gap between him and the group got wider as he moved even faster, trying to catch a few seconds of privacy with me before 50 pairs of ears permanently joined the conversation.

"Shakked!" Rob says with relief.

"Rob!" I answered, "How was the flight?"

"Fine. We're a bit tired but very excited to start our site-seeing right away. We want to make sure we don't miss any of the highlights!" he said.

"Don't worry Rob, you are in good hands. Come, let's go to our bus and get this show on the road!"

Rob's group, like many others, came from a church in Nebraska to visit the Holy Land. They have seven days to go around the country, when the main goal is to cross things off the "Must See" list.

Israel is probably the most interesting place in the world to visit. It may sound pretentious, but I'm not saying it just because this is my job or because this is where I was born. It is mainly because hiding inside Israel is the birthplace of monotheism and the Judeo-Christian culture. Many tour destinations in the world offer monumental sites to visit, but Israel has an ace of spirit. It is a place of God and the soul.

The Holy Land contains over seven thousand years of human history. It is uniquely located as a connecting point between three continents: Africa, Europe, and Asia. This strategic location was the main cause of the "historical chaos" in the land. Every conqueror, army, or merchant had to go through this piece of land to expand to the next continent.

This is why in the chronicles of the land of Israel, we can find conquerors of close geographic proximity, like different Pharaohs and kings of ancient Assyria, but also conquerors who we would never expect to find in the Holy Land of all places, like Richard the Lion Heart, Hulagu Khan, the grandson of Gengihis Khan, and Napoleon Bonaparte. The land never remained under the same regime, or the same religious rule for more than four hundred years, and it was usually far less.

So far Israel sounds like every tour-planner's dream. A land with remains of every culture, religion, and denomination, not to mention the cultural and human abundance of the present. There are so many highlights to see, but that is also the problem. At the end of the day, most visitors will end up seeing pretty much the same sites. It's not because they aren't adventurous enough, or because their tour organizers didn't do their job right. It's simply because there is never enough time to see it all.

In 2009, I finished my mandatory military service in the IDF (Israeli Defense Force) and knew exactly what I wanted to do. I wanted to be a tour guide with all my heart. Maybe it was because my grandfather was also a tour guide and I wanted to follow in his footsteps. Maybe it was because my father took us traveling every weekend to the most beautiful, and secret, corners of the land and made me fall in love with it. Maybe it was because my mother is one of Israel's finest professional storytellers and I wanted to inspire people with mesmerizing stories, too. Or perhaps, it was all of the above.

In any case, three months after I finished my service, I started the Tour Guide Training Program with the Israeli School of Tourism at the University of Haifa.

"Tour guide" doesn't sound like the most glorious profession. It usually brings to mind an image of a museum guide wearing a blue blazer, or some yammery chump quoting entries from Wikipedia seasoned with corny jokes. In Israel, however, the title

"Tour Guide" almost has a halo of prestige to it. The reason why is obvious.

Israel holds within it the holiest places in the world for Judaism and for Christianity. It also holds some of the holiest places to Islam, after Meccah and Medina. Many of these places are sacred not only to more than one denomination, but to more than one religion. The Mount of Olives is a great example. Judaism believes that when the Messiah comes, he will arrive in Jerusalem at the Mount of Olives. Christianity believes that this is where Jesus ascended to heaven from, and where he will return to. Islam believes that this is where doomsday and the final judgement will take place. One single mountain top, being sacred to so many people in so many different ways. As of 2015, Islam makes up 24.1%, and Christianity makes up 31.2% of the world's population[1]. This means that the Mount of Olives is sacred to more than 55% of the world, and that none of them tend to agree with each other. Why don't I count the Jews you ask? Well…0.2% of the world's population is nice…but hardly an impressive piece of data. Maybe we can get a participation ribbon.

No matter their religious affiliation, tour guides must put their personal views and beliefs aside, and be ready to tell the stories and beliefs of everyone involved. To do it even a little bit of justice, a tour guide must be familiar with the history, literature, and theology of all three religions, and their denominations.

Traditions and beliefs aside, Israel is a country under a religious, national, and political conflict. Every bit of land matters and has meaning. Indeed, storytelling in Israel can have fairly explosive consequences. For this reason the Israeli Ministry of Tourism insists on certifying Israeli tour guides. The examinations are of

---

[1] Hackett, C. Mcclendon, D. (2017). *Christians Remain World's Largest Religious Group, But They Are Declining in Europe.* Pew Research Center.

the highest standard and the bar is set very high. After two years of training, many students fail the certification test and have to wait six months until the next one.

The training itself is a once-in-a-life-time experience. For two years straight, we studied everything about the land, its history and its people. In class, we learn about geology, botany, zoology, archeology, theology, geopolitics, architecture, and more. The best part, however, was outside the classroom. Every week for two years, come rain or shine, we would get on a tour bus at 6 a.m., and go on field trips to explore the highlights of Israel, and a long list of significant places that most people never get to visit.

These quick-paced tour days were exhausting. I suppose the fact that we had to follow the tour guide around with note-pads all day to catch every word he said because it might appear on next week's exam may have downgraded the experience.

Nonetheless, these two years were some of the most eye-opening experiences of my life. I learned to experience and read the land like never before. I no longer see a cluster of cities, villages, fields, and some nature. Now everywhere I go, I see layers of history. I see cultures that have flourished, then vanished. I see geological progressions that will keep going for millions of years after we're gone, but most importantly, I see stories.

I couldn't wait to finish the training, get my license, and start showing people all of my favorite places. All the secret corners and hidden stories I never knew existed in my tiny famous country. I had big plans for my future guiding career, but as we say back home, if you want to make God laugh, tell him about your plans. Little did I know at twenty-three years-old and completely new to the guiding business, that a tour guide rarely gets to go to their favorite sites.

Even though traveling is a considerable financial expense, the time is often more valuable than the money. When people come to tour the country, they come for seven to ten days on average. Very few people come back more than once and really explore the land in-depth. Therefore, Israel is not so much a tour-planner's dream as it is a nightmare. There are, as I mentioned, an endless number of things to see, but no matter how much you pack the itinerary, it's never enough.

When we finished our training program, I remember Benny, our program director telling us "Congratulations. Now your real learning can finally begin."

After the two most stressful years of my life, in terms of school demands, that really wasn't what I wanted to hear. Unfortunately, I knew exactly what he meant by that. We studied so much but on many topics, we hardly scratched the surface. It's impossible to learn everything there is to know, otherwise we'd be stuck in tour guide training forever. Alas, such is Israel. Endless in what it has to offer, and a never-ending journey.

It shouldn't have been a surprise for me, when real life ended up being very different from school. Since 2011, when my guiding career started, I can't count the number of times I've visited Masada, the church of Holy Sepulcher, or the Sea of Galilee. They are all still just as magical, as beautiful and as fascinating as they were the first time I visited them. However, I've only gotten to take people to Beit She'arim, one of my favorite sites in Israel, three times. Once when I took my mom, once when my friends from pre-military school asked me to take them to see something cool on a weekend's trip, and once with a group who'd been to Israel many times before and asked me to surprise them. Most of my tourists, I regret to say, never got a chance to visit this incredible place.

Rob and the group followed me to the bus. Once everyone was seated, I took the microphone, introduced myself, and went over the day's itinerary with them.

We had a long drive up north to Nazareth, beginning our journey where Jesus began his. As the bus pulled out, I started the trip as I usually do, by walking up and down the aisle and introducing myself to each member of the group, doing my best to remember their names and form a personal connection with them. One lady was sitting quietly at the front, clutching a book to her chest and balancing three other books on her lap. They were all travel guides to Israel. She introduced herself as Linda, and seemed enthusiastic and eager to talk. It was as if the twenty-hour flight and seven thousand miles were lost on her.

"Someone's been doing some prep work before the trip!" I said, impressed. I love it when people come with prior knowledge as it makes the conversations with them more interesting.

"Yes, I wanted to know as much as I could before I came over." Linda said. "So, I bought different travel guides. I want to know everything there is to know about the Holy Land."

"That's great!" I said, and I meant it.

I was always secretly a bit envious of religious people, who longed to come to Israel and then finally get to come here for the first time.

"Which one's your favorite?" I asked.

"Well, as a matter of fact there is not much of a difference," she said, and I could sense a trace of disappointment in her voice. "I bought a few because I thought each of them would have information about different places, but they're all very similar. Same sites, same recommendations, same information. 'What has been done, will be done again. There is nothing new under the sun.'"

"Ecclesiastes 1:9," I recited the source.

"You know your Bible," she seemed pleased. "Are you a religious Jew?"

"Religion and Jews is a complicated issue. I have my own unique relationship with God. And I do love the Bible, very much," I said, trying to be as honest as I could without getting into a deep philosophical discussion while standing in a moving bus.

"God is in the details," she replied and then added. "I was hoping to find more of these in these travel guides, but maybe I was looking in the wrong place. What's your favorite site in Israel?"

I hate it when visitors ask me this question. Not because it's a bad question to ask, but because I hate disappointing my clients, and answering this question with honesty usually ends up with a disappointed expression on their faces. Since I started guiding, my clients have been asking me this question on almost every tour.

At the beginning of my career, I used to tell them that I have a few favorites on my list, but they are the literal definition of "off the beaten path." They're the places most people don't go to. The places with the really cool stories that never became famous. The real hidden gems of the land. Then I would tell them about one or two of them and describe them in detail.

The next question to follow was usually delivered with anticipation in their eyes "So are we going to go there?"

"Unfortunately, no. These places are not normally on a regular tour itinerary," I'd reply, and if I was lucky, the disappointed expression on their faces was all that I'd have to endure. Had I been less lucky, this would end with them contacting the tour agency to check if the itinerary could take some "last minute changes." The tour agents didn't like that, to say the least. Not to mention that in 99% of the cases, these changes were not possible anyway. An itinerary is like a legal contract, and the highest priority is to fulfill the original plan, to protect the agency from potential lawsuits. Such is business. The product is romantic, the fine print is often not.

The sad outcome of the whole thing is that I stopped answering this question with honesty. When asked "What is your favorite site in Israel?" I'd just pick my favorite one out of the itinerary and make it my answer. However, I couldn't shake off this heavy feeling I had when doing so. First, I hate lying, especially in business. I always try to be completely upfront with people, so this question made me sad. One of the main reasons I became a tour guide was so that I could share the country that I love so much with other people. Israel may be the homeland of the Jews, but it is a spiritual homeland for so many people around the world. It devastated me when I realized that I couldn't share my favorite parts of Israel with the people who came to see it.

"Why do you ask?" I asked, trying to avoid answering. Something told me she was the type of person who dug deeper, and I disliked the thought of lying right off the bat.

"Well", she said with a smile. "I'm hoping you'll have a better answer than these books."

"And what if my answer is also not in our itinerary?" I said, liking her upfront approach. I decided to pay her back with the same honesty.

"Then I should probably start planning my next trip to Israel," she said, and we both laughed.

I was about to gracefully skip answering the question and move on, but then she pulled up her sleeve and showed me a tattoo on the back of her forearm. The tattoo was in Hebrew, and said:

"אין הברכה שורה אלא בדבר הסמוי מן העין"

"That's from the Talmud!" I said, unable to hide my excitement. I recognized this sentence that I had heard from my mother many times before: "A blessing is found only in what is hidden from the eye[2]". This was my mom's reasoning behind making her countless donations to charity anonymous, and the reason she gave me every time she felt I was bragging too loud. Seeing a quote from the Talmud tattooed on an elderly lady's forearm in a Christian tour group was definitely unexpected.

"I thought this was a Christian group," I said, feeling both intrigued and confused.

"I took a DNA test a few years ago and discovered that I have about 7% Ashkenazi Jew in me, mainly from Germany. I've been a Christian my whole life, and Jesus is an inseparable part of my being, but still, in the past few years I've been drawn more and more to study the Jewish wisdom. One day as I was reading, I came across this sentence. Suddenly, I realized that had my Jewish ancestors never left Germany when they did, my family would likely be killed by the Nazis during the holocaust. I never knew my family was Jewish or that they could have been persecuted and killed, until I took the DNA test. It occurred to me that this was a hidden blessing. Since then, I promised myself to always dig deeper, to find the blessings that are hidden from the eye."

"That is an amazing story. Thank you so much for sharing with me. You know what? I think this conversation deserves a better

---

[2] Babylonian Talmud, Tractate Bava Metzia, 42a
(תלמוד בבלי, בבא מציעא דף מב ע"א)

time and place than a bus stand-up talk. I promise I'll tell you about my favorite places in Israel, none of which are in these books."

"I would like that!" she said with clear enthusiasm. I shook her hand and placed my other palm on her tattoo, trying to burn the memory of this conversation into my mind. This was a very special moment for me as a guide.

Linda and I formed a unique relationship during that tour. She always sat at the front of the bus so that we could chat during the long drives, and we spent many of my "windows" during the day, talking about the "hidden gems" of Israel.

Linda may not have realized it at the time, but she gave me a great gift. Going to the same sites day in and day out can wear a guide out pretty quickly. You start to forget the passion you had for your profession when you first started, and start concentrating on the mundane things, like will the line to the cable cart in Masada be long or short or will I get to sleep at home, or in a hotel with the group.

The conversations with Linda got me back to the core passion that brought me into my profession in the first place. I realized there was so much more I wanted to share with my audience than just what was being dictated by the limitations of time, money, and itineraries.

When we arrived at the camel ride, Linda didn't join the group. She said her back probably wouldn't allow it, and stayed behind with me to wait it out. We sat in the cool shade of the Bedouin tent and popped open a couple of cold sodas.

"You know, you should write a travel guide," Linda said.

"Come on, Linda. You said it yourself, 'What has been done, will be done again.' I'm not going to waste my time writing another travel guide that would be added to the pile. People buy travel guides to read about the highlights they are going to see. My job starts when they're already on their tour" I said, tired of the whole thing.

"You're a little bit right and mostly wrong. Most people have a display of travel guides on their bookshelf of places and destinations they'll probably never get to go to. Why do you think they buy them then?" she asked.

"I don't know, but it's funny you mentioned that. I have travel guides in my library of Tuscany, Denmark, South Africa and Jamaica, even though I've never been to those places," I said.

"So why did you buy them?" she asked.

"Because I dream of going there someday, although I really don't see it happening in the near future," I answered.

"Exactly! People buy books of places they DREAM of going to. Maybe someday they'll get to go there and maybe not. Either way, they get to go there in their minds, and that trip is free and endless."

"But these books already exist," I said and then added, "There are an endless number of travel guides about Israel."

"True, but they all try to sell what has already been sold. Same old, same old. Your Israel is fresh," she said.

"Trust me Linda, when it comes to the Holy Land's history, 'fresh' is not the first word that comes to mind," I said and giggled.

"But it is", she continued. "None of these travel guides told me a shred of what is in the stories you told me of what I now look at as 'Shakked's Israel.' I would really like to go there, but moreover, I wish I could read about it. Even if I never get to go there, at least there is more of Israel that I can dream of."

"You make it sound so romantic, and you make a fair point. I'll think about it."

"Atta girl," she said smiling.

We kept on chatting about other topics, but between you and me, I wasn't going to write a travel guide about Israel. I was sincerely flattered by Linda's enthusiasm, but I was working on my Master's degree at the time, and with my busy schedule, I was lucky if I had the time to write a social media status. A book was definitely out of the question.

At the end of the trip, we arranged to meet up in her hotel lobby before her flight. I was waiting when I saw Linda coming over with her pile of Israel travel guides.

"What are these for?" I asked.

"They're for you. You have so much to tell about Israel, more than any of these corny travel guides. I'm giving them to you with a challenge. You must keep them on your work desk at all times, until you write your own travel guide to Israel, with all the hidden gems and secret corners you told me about. Until you do, every time you organize your desk and want to get rid of these books in your way, remember you still have a book to write. Deal?" Linda asked.

I could tell she wasn't joking around when I looked her in the eyes and saw a real spark of faith in them.

"Deal," I said, knowing full well that these books were going to be sitting on my desk for a very long time, collecting dust and taking a back seat to all the papers that I had to write by winter, and all the groups that I had lined up for the spring.

Linda's group left in October 2019, and I cleared my schedule to finish my final papers for graduation.

My plan was to graduate in January 2020, travel through February (the slow season in Israeli tourism), and start a long line of tour groups in March. Instead, the next part is probably a familiar story. March came along and with it, Covid-19, airport shut-downs and a complete halt to tourism in Israel.

As a busy tour guide without a moment to breathe, I suddenly found myself sitting at home, for the first time of my life, with no groups and no income horizon. In the beginning, we thought we were "flattening the curve." People from the tourism industry were sure we would be back to normal in a season or two. So was I. When the crisis revealed itself to be more than a bump in the road, I found myself needing to consider what to do next.

For some people, Covid-19 was somewhat of a blessed challenge. People were forced out of jobs they hated and had to re-calculate their lives. It wasn't necessarily a bad thing. For Israeli tour-guides, however, this wasn't so much the case. For most of us, working this trade was already a dream. Covid-19 meant giving up the dream we were living and finding what to do next to survive.

That's what happened to me.

I found myself sitting at home, going through my bag of tricks, and trying to figure out what to do. I could have gone on a career retraining program, but nothing felt right. I'm a woman of many talents, humility being my greatest one. Still, my one true love and the thing I do best, is talking about Israel, my beloved homeland.

This is my calling, so maybe I needed to change the 'how', but I definitely wasn't going to change the 'what.'

Then, my eyes landed on the pile of Israel travel-guides on my desk, buried under a pile of papers, and the talk with Linda became more vivid than ever.

"The blessing is found only in what is hidden from the eye," the familiar quote from the Talmud rang in my head.

If Israel was now hidden from everyone's eyes, I thought to myself, maybe the blessing could be in bringing it to people in a different way.

At this point in time, the borders of Israel are still closed to foreign citizens. As for myself, I decided that if people can't come to Israel, I will bring Israel all the way to them. So, now I'm traveling the world, speaking to people about Israel, but a talk, like a tour, has the limitations of time, place and money. When I packed my bags to go to the US, my eyes landed again on Linda's travel guides.

She was right all along, I thought. Maybe a book is the best way to bring Israel to everyone who dreams of visiting it. I grabbed the travel guides and packed them too. They added a considerable weight to my suitcase. Good, I thought. This will remind me not to neglect my goal to write that book. It's been six months since I left Israel. I've traveled all over, visiting congregations, and speaking to audiences about Israel.

Between each talk, I write, determined to get rid of the excessive weight of the travel guides. As soon as I started, the stories just poured out of me, and what I forgot or didn't know, I researched, which made the process so much sweeter. It appears that the path to your calling may change, but the calling itself never leaves you.

I couldn't be happier to present my Israel to readers around the world. As for the travel guides, I'm going to drop them off as a donation to the nearest library.

SECRET ISRAEL

SECRET ISRAEL

NAVIGATION

SECRET ISRAEL

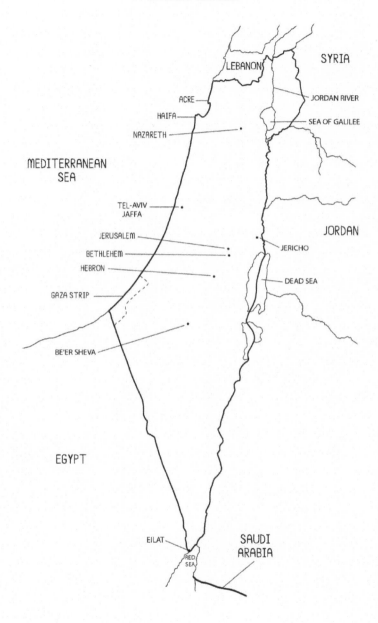

SECRET ISRAEL

PART 1 – THE NORTH

BEIT SHE'ARIM NECROPOLIS

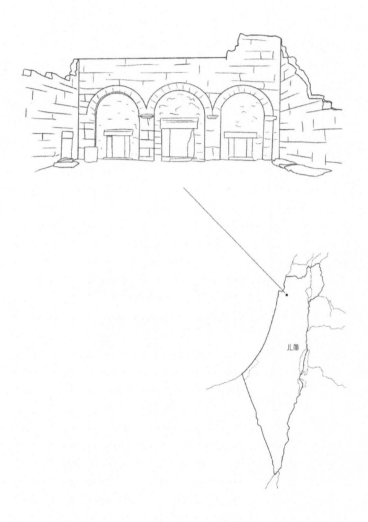

Beit She'arim Necropolis

"The Egyptian, the Babylonian, and the Persian rose, filled the planet with sound and splendor, then faded to dream-stuff and passed away; the Greek and the Roman followed, and made a vast noise, and they are gone; other peoples have sprung up and held their torch high for a time, but it burned out, and they sit in twilight now, or have vanished. The Jew saw them all, beat them all, and is now what he always was, exhibiting no decadence, no infirmities of age, no weakening of his parts, no slowing of his energies, no dulling of his alert and aggressive mind. All things are mortal but the Jew; all other forces pass, but he remains. What is the secret of his immortality?"[1]

- ***Mark Twain***

Beit She'arim in Hebrew means "The house of Gates", and if you ask me, no name could have been more appropriate, for in this place, so I believe, is the gate for the survival of the Jews.

The survival of the Jews is not just physical, for Jews exist today in many physical "forms." In fact, they always did. Judaism was

---

[1] Twain, M. (1899) *Concerning the Jews.* Harper's Magazine.

never "uniformed." Even before the destruction of the Temple in 70 AD, the Jews were fragmented. One of the oldest jokes we tell amongst ourselves is about how even a single Jew in a gentile town must build at least two synagogues: the one he goes to, and the one he'll never set foot in. Today, Jews exist in what often feels like an almost tiresome selection of denominations, points of view and ways of life.

Nonetheless, there are core spiritual elements that Jews share, and in them is a part of what I see as the key to their survival.

Since I started guiding, when people asked me 'What is your favorite site in Israel,' my immediate reply would be "Beit She'arim." Then, they would ask me 'why', and I had no answer. I would put together a few scattered sentences trying to wrap up core ideas and amazing historical developments into one answer. I didn't really know how or where to start. I do know beyond all doubt though, that when I think about Beit She'arim, I get physically excited. I feel my inner butterfly fluttering with the same excitement that gets it to wake up when you listen to great live music.

The essence of the Beit She'arim Necropolis, I believe, is that it cradles in its cold and dead bosom at least one of the keys for the survival of the Jews. However, in order to understand all of that, and in order to hit the Jewish nail of survival right on the head, we must understand exactly what Beit She'arim is. That is where our next story begins.

Provincia Iudaea (Judaea), 70 AD

The Great Rebellion that took place in 70 AD marked the end of an era for Judaism.

Up until that point in time, Judaism, despite the many rifts in its social fabric, revolved around one thing, in one place: serving God in the Temple, in the promised land.

Not all Jews lived in Jerusalem or in the land of Israel, but nonetheless, Jewish life always gravitated towards Jerusalem. Jews who lived outside the land went on pilgrimages to Jerusalem to visit and worship at the Temple three times a year. Moreover, the last ruling about every Jewish matter, proximate or distant, was always done in Jerusalem, based on the verse:

"The law will go out from Zion, the word of the Lord from Jerusalem"

\-   *Isaiah 2:3*

Decision-making and rulings regarding ways of life or legal disputes were done by the Great Assembly, the main legal-body of sages located on the corner of the Temple Mount, in Jerusalem. The Great Assembly was made of one hundred and twenty members, and underneath it were smaller legal bodies, called the Sanhedrin.

A large Sanhedrin had seventy-one members, and a small Sanhedrin had twenty-three members. These Sanhedrins, or legal councils, were a collection of sages, young and old, who'd discuss legal matters according to and in light of the Torah. Much like a judge interprets the constitution to determine a verdict, so did the sages interpret the Torah. These interpretations were done verbally, and are known as the 'Oral Torah' or the 'Oral Law.' The wisdom of the Oral Torah was transferred from one sage to the next, from generation to generation.

The 'Manual' for 'How to be a Jew,' was found in the Tanakh[2], or more precisely, in the Torah[3]. There, Jews could find six hundred and thirteen commandments they were obligated to follow. A third of these commandments revolved around the obligations of the priests in the Temple. The second third dealt with commandments that Jews had to follow regarding the land of Israel such as farming, and more, with specific boundaries for where this land starts and ends. The last third dealt with commandments that Jews had to follow in their daily lives.

After the destruction of the Temple, the Jews faced a new reality. The core of their identity and the center of their life was gone. They were banned from Jerusalem and the Temple was burned and stood in ruins. They lost the core of their being and the heart of their identity.

Under their new circumstances, a group of sages decided to leave the rebels, 'cut their losses,' and try to reconstruct Judaism outside of Jerusalem. The group was made of Pharisee sages who realized that the rebellion and Jerusalem were lost. In their despair, they escaped Jerusalem[4], negotiated with the Romans, and were granted permission to reestablish the Sanhedrin outside of Jerusalem.

The Sanhedrin was reestablished in the city of Yavne, and its sages turned quickly to their most immediate challenge: how to

---

[2] The Hebrew word referring to the Old Testament.

[3] The Hebrew name for the first five books of the Old Testament, from Genesis to Deuteronomy.

[4] In Jerusalem under the Roman siege, Jews could leave and surrender to the Romans, however, the zealots rebels forbade anyone from leaving and threatened to kill anyone attempting to do so.

prevent Judaism from disappearing, now that Jerusalem and the Temple are gone?

The sages were concerned that with the absence of the Jerusalem-authority, instead of one Oral Torah, there would be many, and Judaism would dissolve into tiny communities with nothing to hold them together.

Their first significant act was to substitute the pilgrimage to the Temple. When the Temple stood, Jews were obligated to arrive in Jerusalem for all three pilgrimage festivals, Sukkot, Passover and Shavuot. Now that the Temple was gone and Jews were forbidden from entering Jerusalem, the Sanhedrin decided to put together written prayers that were determined as final and definite in their wording, for every Jew everywhere to follow. This meant that every Jew, everywhere in the world, was quoting the same words in Hebrew in the times determined by the Sanhedrin in Yavne. This tradition continues today.

This act took the realm of holiness from the Sadducees, mainly the priests who worked in the Temple, and expanded it to the personal practice of every Jew in the world. Every Jew, no matter their whereabouts, had the responsibility to practice and follow the rules, to maintain his Judaism for future generations.

The second major act of the Sanhedrin was to send messengers to every Jewish community and invite all of the Jewish sages to assemble and study, at least for a while, in Yavne. This act established the hegemony of the new Sanhedrin over the Jewish communities around the world, even exiled from Jerusalem.

The sages who came to Yavne studied the new rules and then went back to manage their communities. More often than not, they were outside of the land of Israel. Soon enough, local sages had to make decisions and developed debates on their own. The hegemony of Yavne was hard to maintain, given the poor means of communication available and the lack of necessity to arrive in Jerusalem, in the absence of the Temple.

In addition, during the years 132 to 136, another rebellion was ignited by some of the Jews in the province of Judaea, the Bar Kokhba Revolt. This rebellion was started in an attempt to reverse the outcome of the Great Rebellion, restore Jewish dominance in Jerusalem, rebuild the Temple, break the Roman burden off of the back of the Jews and establish an independent autonomy in the land of Israel.

For a while, the rebellion seemed to work, but it didn't last. Soon enough, the Roman army crushed the rebellion, and this time they made sure to clear the Judaea region of Jews. The outcomes of the rebellion were disastrous. Hundreds of Jewish villages were simply erased, hundreds of thousands were killed and according to Roman sources, so many Jews were taken captive and made into slaves that the price of a Jewish slave in the Roman market was cheaper than the cost of feeding a horse once.[5]

To prevent the Jews from having any future hope of returning to Jerusalem, the Roman Emperor Hadrian built a Roman city in its place, putting temples for the Roman gods on top of the Temple Mount. To erase any trace of Jewish presence from the land, he also changed the name of the province from Provincia Iudaea (Judaea) to Provincia Syria Palestina (after the ancient Philistines who used to live in the area centuries beforehand).

Jezreel Valley, Galilee, Provincia Syria Palestina, Roman Regime, 136 AD

In the chaos, the Sanhedrin abandoned Judaea, which was cleared of its Jewish presence for the most part, and moved to the Galilee,

---

[5] L. Dindrof. I, Bonn. (1832). *Chronicon Paschale*, ed. (p. 474)

where some Jews who didn't take part in the rebellion were still allowed to live. Soon enough, the Sanhedrin established its new residency in the Galilee town of Beit She'arim, in Jezreel Valley.

The destruction of the Temple followed by the banishment of Jews from Judaea, along with the distance from the Jewish communities worldwide, weakened the hegemony of the Sanhedrin in Israel and the risk of Judaism dissolving into fractions of Judaism with no unifying force, became greater than ever.

Approximately one hundred years after the destruction of the Temple, the president of the Sanhedrin, known by the name Rabbi Yehuda HaNasi[6], was laboring over a project that would change the face of Judaism and grant it a tool for physical and spiritual survival. To prevent the Jewish wisdom from being lost, Rabbi[7] (Rabbi Yehuda HaNasi in short) took it upon himself to write down the records of the Sanhedrin, the rules and decisions, and to unify them into one definitive version in a collection of six books, more commonly known as the 'orders,' of the Mishnah.

The Six Orders of the Mishnah provided a complete set of rules that every Jew could live by. Rabbi then sent messengers to spread the word of the new document formed by the Sanhedrin of Israel, and made sure it was accepted in every Jewish community as the new creed to live by.

The Mishnah became a foundational document for Jews worldwide, and established its gatherer and editor, Rabbi Yehuda HaNasi, as one of the most famous Rabbis to ever live.

---

[6] HaNasi - Hebrew for 'the president', Nasi was the title of the president of the Sanhedrin.

[7] 'Rabbi' is the commonly short name used to address Yehuda HaNasi (exclusively). No other Jewish Rabbi or sage is addressed just by the name 'Rabbi' without a name added.

When Rabbi's health deteriorated, he moved to a nearby town called Tzipori, which was located on the top of the mountain, rather than down in the Jezreel Valley. The move was done with the hope that it would benefit Rabbi's health, and the entire Sanhedrin moved there with him. Despite the move, Rabbi sensed that his death was near, and made arrangements. He asked that his burial would be "Nekuva BaAretz," meaning a hole in the ground, named his son Nasi (president) of the Sanhedrin after him, and asked that a Yeshiva[8] would be built above his burial place[9].

Beit She'arim existed until the 4th Century AD, and the reason for its destruction was most probably another rebellion of the Jews against the Romans, known as the Gallus Revolt of 351 AD.

So far, the story of Beit She'arim is rather dull. It's a place where an important Rabbi did something important, and then was buried there after his death. Nothing too interesting to write home about.

Jezreel Valley, Galilee, British Mandate of the Land of Israel, 1936

"How was the road?" Alexander Zaid asked when he finally met with his old friend on the main road.

The young archeologist climbed off the wagon, carrying a duffle bag with some clothes, a briefcase containing his notes, and a large bundle of old books tied together with a thin rope. He was steaming under his buttoned shirt and sweater vest, his forelock

---

[8] A **Yeshiva** (from Hebrew, literally means 'sitting' or 'a place for sitting'), is commonly used until today to describe an educational institution for Jewish religious studies, however, in the time of Rabbi Yehuda HaNasi, it is more probable to assume that the term was used to describe the sitting place of the Sanhedrin.

[9] Amit, H. Amit, D. (2005). *Marei Makom, Reference Points, Traveling with the Jewish Sources in Northern Israel*. Yad Yizhak Ben Zvi. Jerusalem. Pp. 76-87

was dripping sweat over his face, and his thick round eyeglasses were foggy. Nonetheless, he had a big smile on his face and he seemed full of energy.

"Bumpy, steamy and gorgeous. You look well old friend!" Benjamin Mazar answered and meant it.

He always admired Zaid who was leading by example, living the life of a pioneer and 'redeeming' the barren parts of the land of Israel with farming, herding and guarding. Alexander was tall, broad shouldered and muscular. His grown yellow forelock and blue eyes glistened in the sun. Benjamin looked at him with 90% admiration and 10% jealousy, given that while under the beating sun Zaid looked like the salt of the earth, in comparison, Benjamin thought he looked like a hot wet mess. He shouldn't have worn this stupid sweater.

Alexander looked at his old friend and felt curiosity burning inside him. He loved his life of hard labor and connection to the land. Benjamin however, had the kind of connection Zaid could never have. He could look at the land and historical events would rise before his eyes. He knew the scriptures almost by heart and the land told him secrets in a language only he could interpret. When Zaid found that ancient place on his lands, he knew he had discovered something big, something meaningful, but he didn't have the knowledge to understand what it was. He burned with curiosity and couldn't wait for Benjamin to come examine it.

"Let's go, Zipporah is waiting for us" he said and handed Benjamin the reins to the second horse he brought with him. Then he took the duffle bag from Benjamin's hand to tie to the saddle.

Benjamin climbed onto the horse's back and Zaid climbed on the back of the other one and secured the gun in his belt. Hostile ambushes weren't a rarity, and since Zaid and his family lived alone in a territory surrounded by Arabs, he was always on guard.

Benjamin steadied the books on the front of the saddle and said to Zaid "Each man and his weapon of choice!" Alexander laughed and clicked his tongue and the horses started moving.

Alexander Zaid[10]

Benjamin may have joked, but he knew very well the dangers lurking for two Jewish riders in Jezreel Valley in 1936. The violence between Jews and Arabs had already claimed too many victims, and he had no desire to contribute to the statistics.

"I am happy you decided to come my friend", Alexander said as the horses started climbing the grass-covered hills.

"After what I read in your letter I had to come and see for myself," Benjamin said. "Something tells me this is something big. So tell me, how did you find it?"

"I was laying foundations for a new structure when suddenly I discovered an opening to a cave," Alexander said. "I took a torch and went inside. The walls were roughly hewn and I found myself in an endless maze underground. There is more, but I'd rather you see it with your own eyes."

---

[10] Source: Public Domain, Bet Alon Archives.

"Did you see any symbols or inscriptions you could recognize? Could you identify a certain culture or nation who's been there?" Benjamin was thirsty to find out.

"Patience my friend", Alexander said. "First, we must make it safely to the house, and before we head to the caves we must let Zipporah feed you tea and raisin cakes, or I won't hear the end of it."

"I do miss Zipporah's raisin cakes," Benjamin said, and after a moment of silence he started chuckling.

"What's so funny?" Alexander said.

"I just realized that despite your national reputation for being the bravest and fiercest Hebrew Guard in the land, the one person to penetrate your reign of terror, is armed with raisin cakes."

"Oh, it's not the raisin cakes I fear my friend, it's the fearless woman who made them and the tongue she was blessed with," Alexander said. They laughed together, and made their way to the lone house on the hills of Sheikh Ibreik.

Zipporah greeted them in the yard outside the house while she was trying to get a gelding to settle down.

"Benjamin, you look great!" she said and added "tea and cake are inside, and don't let this one take you exploring before you're rested. I'm off to Nahalal to get supplies, see you boys later tonight."

Zipporah got up on the gelding, started galloping and disappeared behind the trees.

As much as he appreciated her hospitality and concern, Benjamin had no intention of resting. He was anxious. The road from Haifa to Jezreel valley seemed to last forever. A hunch kept telling him that a big adventure was ahead, and he was eager to get going.

Zipporah Zaid[11]

Alexander read his mind. As soon as Zipporah was out of sight he turned to Benjamin and said "I'll tie the horses and fix us some torches. Put your luggage inside, grab the raisin cakes and I'll meet you on top of the hill. Oh, and don't forget to rumple the bed's sheets in the mainroom, to establish that you are well rested," he winked at him with a mischievous smile.

Soon enough, they were both going down the hill behind the Zaid's family cabin, toward a cave opening that was hidden behind the high grass. Alexander went in first, his torch lighting the way. Benjamin followed him, touching the cave's chalky walls. It was obvious that the walls were man made.

'This isn't a hiding cave or a storing facility', he thought to himself.

The heavy smell of chalk dust in his nostrils mixed with the flavor of Zipporah's raisin cake that was still fresh on his tongue. His

---

[11] Zipporah Zaid on her horse. Contribution of Tali Zaid of the Zaid family house to the public domain.

heart was beating fast. Another turn, and then another. The space suddenly got big, like a wide and spacious corridor carved into the hill. Along the walls, Benjamin saw long long lines of sarcophaguses[12]. They were all carved out of limestone as well, and seemed like each weighed between four to five tons.

Sarcophaguses, Beit shearim, 2021.[13]

Benjamin stopped to pay closer attention. His hands stroked the limestone lids and he noticed that someone broke a big piece of it. Not big enough to take the corpse out, but just big enough to slide a hand in, and pull out anything valuable. 'Grave robbers,' he thought with disappointment. Not that the corpses minded, he knew, but for an archeologist, the treasures that could be found in sarcophaguses might have tremendous value for research. In ancient times, the dead would often be buried with their jewelry,

---

[12] Limestone funeral receptacle for corpses. The name comes from Greek and stands for "flesh-eating". The corpses would be placed in the sarcophagus and sealed with a lid made of limestone as well, for the flesh to dissolve. Outside the sarcophaguses there would sometimes be carvings of different decorations and or mythological characters.

[13] Source: Pikiwiki photo stock. Credit: Shlomit Mesika, 2021.

and even with money, to pay off the ferryman who takes them to the 'other side.' Benjamin's disappointment didn't last too long, as he couldn't see anything anymore. Alexander kept moving forward, carrying the torch with him.

"Alexander, wait!" he called after him and his voice echoed in the cave. "I want to examine these sarcophaguses!"

"Benjamin? where are you?" Alexander called, as he was already further along in the cave, and took a turn. "Stay with me. It is easy to lose your way in here[14]. Most of these were already broken into. Look - ," he said, holding the torch near an arch-shaped opening carved into the main corridor wall, leading to one crypt out of many.

There were a few sarcophaguses with no decorations on them. In the light of the torch Benjamin could see faded engravings in a language he didn't recognize right away. However, the most obvious thing was the broken segment in the lid of each and every sarcophagus. All were broken into, robbed.

"We're in a crypt, a massive one, but I still don't know what kind," Benjamin said and took two steps into the room to take a closer look, when he felt Alexander's heavy hand on the back of his shoulder.

"Oh, but I do," Alexander said. "You can examine these later. There are dozens of them in this cave. Come with me, I didn't tell you about the last part, I wanted you to see with your own eyes."

---

[14] Anonymous. (1975). *At Dawn - Diary Chapters*. Translation of Alexander Zaid's diary from Russian to Hebrew. Original Publisher: Am Oved. Electronic Version: Ben-Yehuda Project.

Benjamin's heart was beating. This, the action and connection, is what gave him a sense of mission.

In Germany, he studied history, geography and archeology at the University of Berlin. The entire time though, he couldn't wait to join his parents and siblings, who had already established their home in the land of Israel. His father had a 'good nose for danger,' and as a child he remembered well how they had to move again, and again. Be it from the German invasion in World War I that drove his family from Poland to Krim, or the communists who drove them to Warsaw.

When the British mandate published the Balfour Declaration, stating that Britain supports the establishment of a national home for the Jews in the land of Israel, his father didn't need further persuasion. After feeling like there was no place safe for them in the world, the hope for a national home in the land of Israel no less, was the modern manifestation of 'the promised land.'

After they arrived in the land of Israel, they never moved anywhere else. The move had three points of attraction for Benjamin. Uniting with his family, and being an active part of the Zionist dream were the first obvious two. The third however, was a fulfillment of pioneering like no other. His interest in history and archeology along with his Zionistic affiliations, drove his fascination with the land of Israel and the light it could pour on Jewish history and its connection to the Holy Land.

Benjamin Mazar wasn't the only archeologist who was eager to excavate the treasures of the Holy Land. Throughout the 19th Century, there were many in Europe who took an interest in the region, specifically due to its biblical affinities. Despite their high interest, there wasn't much that could be done with satisfying the European archeologists' thirst for excavations and findings. The Ottoman Empire had ruled the land since 1517 and treated any request to dig in its territory with significant suspicion, and often refused the requests.

In 1918, after the final elimination of the Ottoman Empire from the "board game" of the world's superpowers, the British Mandate, under the supervision of the League of Nations (which became the United Nations after World War II), took its place in the land of Israel. The British mandate named the region "Palestine," after the name 'Provincia Syria Palaestina," given to the land by the Romans[15]. The British Empire was extremely invested in the research of the region and what it had to offer, financially and historically. With the establishment of their regime, archeological excavations spread in the Holy Land faster than a plague.

With the support of the British Mandate to excavate in the land of Israel, Benjamin was thrilled to start revealing the treasures the land had to offer. In 1928, he graduated his studies and joined his family under the British Mandate in the land of Israel. Now, eight years later, he found himself following Alexander Zaid, one of the greatest pioneers the land had ever known, into the depths of a giant crypt.

Benjamin followed Alexander through the cave's corridor and into a main hall. There, deep in the belly of the hill, in the dancing light of the flame, he saw a giant Menorah[16] carved into the wall. The Menorah was taller than Alexander, who was himself the size of a Cossack. This was a gigantic Jewish crypt, like nothing he

---

[15] The name was chosen in place of the name "Provincia Iudaea" (Judaea"), to disconnect the Jewish heritage from the land after the rebellion the Jews picked against the Roman empire in 66 AD. The name "Palaestina" and later on "Palestine", is based on the link the empires of the ancient world often made between this region and the long lost nation of the Philistines, who disappeared completely from the region in the 7th century BC.

[16] A Jewish symbol, the oil lamp of the Temple.

had ever known or studied about before. They both stood there for a long moment, taking in the sight and the excitement.

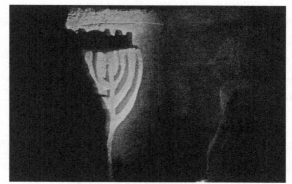

The Menorah of Beit She'arim, 2021.[17]

"Thank you for inviting me to see it first," Benjamin said.

"Who else but you my friend," Alexander answered and added, "Well, we are definitely home".

Come evening, Zaid almost had to drag Benjamin out of the cave before dark. The Zaid family lived alone on the hills of Sheikh Ibreik, and the dangers were plentiful. Zaid worked for the Jewish National Fund as a guard on the lands that they purchased, and the proximity to the Arab and Bedouin villages was dangerous, especially for a family on its own. Not to mention for a lone archeologist, should he end up wandering around the hills at night alone, searching for his way back to the house.

That night, Benjamin sent telegrams to the heads of the Israel Exploration Society and other scholars whom he thought could help. In the meantime, he was invited by Alexander and Zipporah to stay in their home, while he explored the crypts further.

---

[17] Source: Pikiwiki photo stock. Credit: Shlomit Mesika, 2021.

While Alexander worked the fields by day and guarded them by night, Benjamin spent every day in the caves from dawn till dusk, collecting, sketching, copying, writing and revealing an entire system piece by piece. Come evening, Alexander would enter the cave and start searching between the carved rooms until he could find the flickering light of Benjamin's oil lamp. He would find him on his knees in the dirt, and had to beg him to call it a day and join the family for dinner.

One night, after dinner was done with, Alexander didn't go back outside to ride his horse and guard the fields in the valley like every night. After the kids took to their beds and Zipporah was busy in the kitchen, he turned to Benjamin and said "I am not leaving this house until you tell me what is the place we found."

Benjamin Mazar in the excavations of Beit She'arim, 1936.
In the background the entrance doors to the cave, with "nails" carved in stone.[18]

---

[18] Source: The archives of the Israeli Governmental Office of Journalism.

"Well," Benjamin said, "If I am not wrong, and I definitely could be wrong," he kept going, "I think we found the ancient city of Beit She'arim."

"So, what are all these sarcophaguses doing down there? Is it the cemetery of the sages of the Sanhedrin?" Zaid tried guessing.

"Yes, and no," Benjamin answered and turned to his notes. "You see, according to the scriptures, towards the end of his life, Rabbi's students buried him here in Beit She'arim. It says that Rabbi asked for his burial to be 'Nekuva BaAretz,' meaning to be buried in a hole in the ground, with no monuments or tombs built upon it, following the popular notion of that time:

"You don't build monuments for the righteous. Their words and actions are their commemoration[19]*."*

Down in the crypt however, there is a huge assembly of carved stone coffins. Sarcophaguses of different shapes and sizes, with and without decorations. They are all definitely made for Jews to be placed in, but some even had carved decorations of scenes from Greek mythology on them, despite the explicit ban from the ten commandments

"You shall not make for yourself an image..."

- ***Exodus 20:4***

"Look," he continued. "I copied these texts from different coffins in different rooms in the cave. There are Jews here from Tyre, Syria, Babylon, Anatolia, even from southern Arabia[20]. I

---

[19] Jerusalem Talmud, Shkalim Tractate, Chapter 2 Halacha 5

[20] Gabai M. Yitzhaki, G. (2001). *The New Israel Guide.* Volume 4. Keter Publishin House. Jerusalem. Pp. 57-65.

didn't find the burial place of Rabbi, but other rabbis from the Sanhedrin who lived after him are definitely buried here. It appears that other than them, very rich people, doctors, heads of synagogues, sailors and merchants paid good money to be brought and buried in the land of Israel after they died. I've found engravings in over twenty languages so far, and I am not even close to being finished. Somehow, after the death of Rabbi, a huge burial facility developed here. My guess is that there are probably more caves than this one."

***

Benjamin Mazar was right. His excavation of Beit She'arim is considered to be the first Jewish excavation in the land of Israel.[21] The discovery was remarkable. The site of Beit She'arim today contains several caves, and each cave can contain one hundred carved stone coffins or burial rooms. The cave Alexander Zaid found alone contains about one hundred and thirty-five sarcophaguses. In the entire site, inscriptions and engravings were found in over three hundred languages, indicating a mind-blowing historical fact - Beit She'arim revealed itself to be an "international burial factory" of sorts. It may sound strange, but that's because it *is* strange. There is no equivalent to that, as far as I know, in the ancient world.

Imagine that every Catholic around the world, given that he or she could afford such an expensive whim, would pay unimaginable sums of money to have their body shipped, post mortem, often beyond the seas, to be buried in Rome.

Beit She'arim became a place for Jews of different and distant regions, who spoke different languages, to invest their money in

---

[21] Safrai, Z. (2001). *The History and Importance of Beit Shearim*. Gatherings of the Land of Israel. Ariel 147-148. Jerusalem. Pp. 11-25.

shipping their body to Beit She'arim for their final rest. What was the reason for it?

Well, a simple reason revealed itself during the excavation. In a cave that is now called Cave Number 14, the archeologists discovered what they had been hoping to find with all of their might.

The entrance to the cave was glorious. Three arches at the entrance were carved into the mother rock, it had the feeling of an entrance to a sacred place. The doors were something I'd never seen before - they were made completely out of limestone, which is very impractical for a door, but were carved to seem as if they were made out of wood, to such an exact level of carving as to have nail-like bumps in the rock.

The entrance to the burial caves, 2018.[22]

To enter the great structure through the stone door, you must bend over. Some traditions would claim that this was done in order to

---

[22] Source: Pikiwiki photo stock. Credit: Dr. Avishai Teicher, 2018.

force every living person to bow in respect for the dead upon entry.

At the end of the cave are two graves, unlike any other coffins or sarcophaguses found in any other cave in the entire burial site. The two graves are dug into the ground.

The grave of Rabbi Yehuda HaNasi. Cave 14, Beit She'arim, 2018.[23]

On the walls of the cave, Hebrew inscriptions were found that mentioned the names of two of Rabbi Yehuda HaNasi's sons, and one of his students, all three were described in the scriptures and named by him as his successors before his death.

Finally, above the giant cave are the remains of an ancient public structure of sorts, from the 3rd Century AD, that was used for assemblies. This was apparent from the traces of stone carved benches found in it. All of these findings indicated that this is most likely the resting place of Rabbi Yehuda HaNasi, the creator of the Mishnah, and his wife[24].

---

[23] Source: Pikiwiki photo stock. Credit: Dr. Avishai Teicher, 2018.
[24] Amit, H. Amit, D. (2005). *Marei Makom, Reference Points. Traveling with the Jewish Sources in Northern Israel*. Yad Yizhak Ben Zvi. Jerusalem. Pp. 76-87

The answer to the question "What brought so many Jews from the diaspora to invest unimaginable sums of money in their deaths and have their corpses shipped to be buried in Beit She'arim" is an easy one. These people wanted to be buried next to Rabbi, probably because of his exceptional greatness.

Yeah...no.

This answer was far from satisfying. With all due respect to Rabbi's greatness, I hardly see how a rich Jew, be he a doctor, a merchant or the head of a synagogue in south Arabia, would invest his money in being buried far away from his family, instead of leaving the money for his family and being buried close to them. There has to be more to it.

My first visit to Beit She'arim was an experience I will forever remember. It was part of my Tour Guide Training Program, which to my great delight, made sure to take us to all the important sites, even if they weren't a part of the "Highlight" list. The visit left a great impression on me and to this day I regret that it isn't a part of every standard tour. The sad truth is that I can count the number of times I got to guide in Beit She'arim on less than three fingers.

The feeling I had when I visited is hard to describe. I kept going there by myself, stopping there on my way back and forth, just to visit it again. I just wanted to see the crypts and the tomb of Rabbi one more time. It was engraved in me and soon became my favorite site in Israel and I didn't know how to explain it. I am sure my affection for the dark and mysterious definitely played a part in why the ancient catacombs are my favorite site. I could add my strong love of the romanticism that encompassed the stories of the first pioneers who settled and guarded the land to this place. Alexander Zaid was also definitely a personal hero of mine.

These are all perfectly good reasons, but none of them reflected my very subjective, yet very strong feeling that I was missing something. No site moved me like Beit She'arim did.

It felt like I knew a lot, but was missing something big.

In life it is important to admit when you are off key. To understand what it was that I was missing, I turned to the only person in the land that listening to him speak gave me the same feeling that Beit She'arim gave me. My teacher, friend, and the most sinful Rabbi I ever had the good fortune to encounter, Yaron Ben Ami.

Pre-Military Training Program, Kibbutz Maagan Michael, Spt. 2006

We were sitting in class, waiting for our lecturer for "The History and Antiquities of the Jewish People" to enter the class. It was our second day in the training program and none of us knew what to expect. Suddenly, the space of the open door was completely filled by a giant man who had to bend over to pass through it.

He was six foot ten, but his giant Jewfro[25] made him look taller. His dense and curly hair was so long it floated around the sides of his head and shoulders, making his giant silhouette even more intimidating.

Between the two sides of massive hair, way up there on that giant head, you could see a pair of glasses and a goatee. He was broad shouldered and wore black jeans and a black shirt. A silver earring dangled off of his left ear and a bead necklace with a skull at its end decorated his chest. He took heavy steps in his giant buckled

---

[25] A joke name for an Afro hair style on a Jew

58

black leather boots as he walked into the classroom. He had the deep voice of a friendly giant, as long as he didn't roar.

I looked at him and my eyes opened wide. He seemed as if he came from a parallel universe of larger, badass people. Nothing about him indicated that he should be allowed to walk freely among the rest of society, and without a leash no less. Although I doubt you could find anyone who'd agree to hold on to the other end of that leash. As he took his place near the board, my thoughts alternated between 'Wow, this guy is seriously badass' and 'I want to get as far away from his bad side as I possibly can.' His palms were the size of dinner plates, and one of them had long nails. 'He must play guitar,' I thought.

Yaron Ben Ami didn't need to open his mouth to make an impression, but when he did - he captured my admiration forever.

My dad always said "Don't admire anyone. You can appreciate someone's work or talent, you can like them, but don't admire anyone or put them on a pedestal. That's when trouble starts."

Since then, I've always tried to find bad qualities in people who capture my admiration as a mental exercise. In the case of Yaron, there were many, and I am sure he'd gladly testify that they are all very true and that he's proud of each and every one of them.

I half-expected a Rabbi or a college professor to walk into the classroom. I'd never imagined that the best teacher I would ever have for Jewish history would be a giant, blues singing pirate with a Jewfro. From there, the story only gets better.

"I am here to tell you the story of Judaism, which is the most badass story in the whole wide world, or at the very least, more badass than rock'n'roll" was the first thing we heard him say. I knew right there and then that we would get along great.

When religious people talk about their religion, they usually have the light of devotion, the shine of definite truth screaming from their eyes. You can see them tripping. Religion is love and hate and passion and sacrifice. It is all of the zestful promises life can make you. It is a feeling of meaning like no other.

I wasn't brought up religious, but my connection to Judaism, my land and my people was an inherent part of me since childhood. This is probably why I never sought Jewish growth among Rabbis. Nonetheless, my heritage made my heart race and my blood rush. I am willing to bet that when I discover a new juicy piece of history, my pupils get dilated. When I started diving into history it wasn't through religion, but through the secular-traditional system I grew up in. During those years, I met many secular scholars who studied Judaism their whole lives. The vast majority of them, though, were lacking that light of passion in their eyes. They made my beloved yummy history into a gray and dry list of events. Listening to them was tidies, and they held the great talent of putting me to sleep every time they started talking.

Yaron on the other hand, was the perfect secular Judaism prodigy.

He had just that missing element, the one that makes people pray with intent or that makes people dance in a rock concert, the one that makes people on psychedelic drugs feel like they are one with all of creation. He was the living embodiment of a rockstar devil, who knew every book of Jewish wisdom, Jewish sage or Jewish poet.

Yaron knew how to weave between them and blow your mind with lofty and sinful ideas. He knew how to make history sing the blues in a sound so profound you'd think the angels came down to earth to recruit you to the dark side. In his brilliance, he beat everyone to the punchline, and did it so well all I could do was remind myself to close my mouth as I memorized the lines. I learned from him that learning the story of your heritage from a demon makes it that much tastier, and to hell with your health. God doesn't like life to be pretty and perfect and boring. That's why he makes sure to throw curveballs at us every once in a while.

Learning Judaism from Yaron was one of the most formative experiences of my life and to this day I hold a debt of gratitude to him I don't think I can ever repay.

I've always loved Israel, and always knew I lived in a cool place. However, it was Yaron Ben Ami who proved to me that I was right, that this is not just a cool place. It is the coolest and most badass place on earth. I will be forever grateful to Yaron. For there is nothing in this world I love more than being right.

Pre-Military Training Program, Kibbutz Maagan Michael, 2010

Like the vast majority of young Jews in Israel, I joined the military right at the end of my training program. As soon as I finished my mandatory service, I was lucky enough to be offered a position as a counselor and staff member in the same pre-military training program. To my great joy, this made Yaron and I colleagues. That also meant that I had him 'on site' to do some digging about anything that had to do with 'the deeper side' of Jewish history.

One day at noon, Yaron had just finished teaching and I took the rest of the day off. I waited for the last student to leave the premises and head over to their next lesson. Yaron was sitting on the rock outside the classroom, smoking his "after-class" cigarette.

"We need to talk," I said, coming from my hiding place around the building.

"What about?" Yaron asked.

"Beit She'arim," I said.

"Now?" Yaron seemed on the fence.

"I bring tribute," I said and pulled a bottle of wine from behind my back.

"Now suddenly seems like a perfect time", Yaron was hooked. *"Wine that maketh glad the heart of man[26],"* he quoted, and followed me to the library. It was one of my favorite places to have a drink. Fine wine pairs well with Messianic narratives.

"What am I missing about the punch of the Beit She'arim Necropolis?" I asked, pouring the wine into two glasses.

"Beit She'arim is the gateway to the afterworld. In Beit She'arim the importance of Israel and Jerusalem is moved from this world to the next," he said, sipping his wine.

"This is good wine," I said. "So, you're going to have to be more specific."

Yaron laughed and explained, "After Rabbi died around 220 AD, the institution of the presidency of the Sanhedrin slowly crumbled. There were a few good reasons for that. For starters, the leadership was passed from father to son, and it is hard to maintain a strong leadership when it travels along a bloodline. Second, times in the land of Israel were hard. The Romans weren't always kind with the Jews, whom they now called rebellious and dangerous to peace in the empire. You'd also want to add the establishment and growth of a huge Jewish center in Babylon to all of that, which

---

[26] Psalms 104:15

was a great threat to the Sanhedrin's hegemony in the land of Israel."

"Because there is no more Jerusalem. So it doesn't matter where the spiritual center is?" I asked.

"Yes, that, and the fact that Babylon was under the Sasanian Empire's regime, it belonged to Persia. Under their rule, life was much more comfortable for the Jews, and we're approaching the golden age of Judaism in Babylon," Yaron said.

"That gave us the Babylonian Talmud?" I added.

"Yes," Yaron said. "It was far more successful than it's prototype, the 'Jerusalem Talmud' that was written in the land of Israel in the city of Tiberias. It was a few centuries later, but it is definitely the peak of Judaism in Babylon, which was built upon centuries of a growing Jewish power in that region. The Jews of Babylon took it and made it that much better. The Jewish presence never disappeared from the land of Israel, but the significance of it faded. It paled next to the growing power of Judaism in Babylon. With Jerusalem gone and the majority of Jews living outside of Israel, what did the Sanhedrin in the land of Israel have to offer?"

I finally understood.

"I think I see where you're going with this," I said. "This 'burial factory' is basically an endeavor to increase the importance of the land of Israel over Babylon? To influence the Jews to return to it in the absence of Jerusalem and the Temple?"

"It is the one ace Babylon would never have up its sleeve," he said. "We cannot offer you the Holy Land here and now. The rebellions made sure of that. There was no more physical existence to Jews in the land of Israel. Not a solid one. What we *can* offer though, is the Holy Land in the afterlife".

"Is this where the concept of 'burrow-reincarnation comes from?'" I asked, and now I was truly excited.

"Of that, I am not one hundred percent sure, but if it is, and you are right, it means that Beit She'arim is the gateway to the afterlife, and to Jewish mysticism".

"Give me a few minutes," I said. "Here, have a drink," I poured another glass and headed to the computer to find the right reference to the right book. After a short search, thank you technology, I found what I was after. Burrow reincarnation was a concept first introduced in Jewish scriptures by a sage that lived shortly after Rabbi Yehuda HaNasi died. The existence of the afterworld was a Pharisee view long beforehand, but the connection between resurrection and the Holy Land lay, to the best of my understanding, in Beit She'arim, with the thinning Jewish hegemony of the Sanhedrin.

"Here", I said, "look!" I placed the book under Yaron's nose and almost spilled his wine.

"Rabbi Elazar said: The dead of the lands outside of Eretz Yisrael will not come alive and be resurrected in the future, as it is stated: "And I will set glory in the land of the living" (Ezekiel 26:20)...And according to the opinion of Rabbi Elazar, will the righteous outside of Eretz Yisrael not come alive at the time of the resurrection of the dead? Rabbi Ile'a said, They will be resurrected by means of rolling, i.e., they will roll until they reach Eretz Yisrael, where they will be brought back to life. Rabbi Abba Salla Rava strongly objects to this: Rolling is an ordeal that entails suffering for the righteous. Abaye said, Tunnels are prepared for them in the ground, through which they pass to Eretz Yisrael."

- ***Babylonian Talmud, Tractate Ketubot, Page 111a.***

"Now tell me, if you were positive that you were a righteous person, wouldn't you want to avoid the suffering of rolling through tunnels underground in order to make it for resurrection in the Holy Land?" Yaron laughed.

"Now that will justify a good investment," I said, relieved. Finally, I understood. "The Jews in the Galilee developed a 'burial factory' in Beit She'arim, revolving the desire of Jews around the world to take part in the resurrection. What better place to do that than around a place that already has a halo of righteousness and glory to it, like the burial of Rabbi Yehuda HaNasi?".

"There is more than that," Yaron added. "Always follow the money. The systems required for the applications of the Mishnah were very costly. You must make copies, or train messengers who learn the entire Mishnah by heart and teach it to Jews in the communities outside the land of Israel. This costs a lot of money."

"And an international burial factory to avoid burrow reincarnation is a great way to make money?" I asked, but already knew the answer. The death industry of Beit She'arim was very successful, at least for a while.

"The battle between Judaism in Babylon and Judaism in the land of Israel, is a battle between a social, legal and political order on one hand, and mysticism on the other," Yaron concluded.

"Talmud versus redemption?" I wanted to make sure I understood him correctly.

"Mysticism always mirrors its era. People can endure tremendous suffering, but they hate suffering for no reason. Mysticism gives meaning to suffering. You suffer in this life, but you will be rewarded in the next. The search for meaning is the source of a lot of suffering in human existence," Yaron explained his view of things.

"So who won?" I asked.

"Mysticism, big time. Beit She'arim is an archeological expression of the Holy Land's pre-kabalistic Jewish mysticism, the kind you can read about in Hekhalot Literature[27]. Jewish mysticism is the cradle of Hasidic Judaism, and without Hasidic Judaism, there is no Zionism," Yaron stated and emptied his third wine glass.

"So the key for Jewish survival lies in Beit She'arim?" I asked with excitement.

"For this discussion, you're going to need a bottle of Whiskey," Yaron flipped the bottle of wine into the glass to indicate it was empty, and we both had a good laugh.

***

Yaron's words, "People can endure tremendous suffering, but they hate suffering for no reason," stuck with me for a while.

They were based on Nietzsche's *'He who has a why to live for, can bear almost any how.'* I couldn't help but think about the famous book *"Man's Search for Meaning - Introduction to Logotherapy"* by Victor Frenkle.

Frenkle was an Austrian Jew who worked as a psychiatrist until he ended up in Auschwitz during World War II. In the book, Frenkle survived the horrors he endured by focusing his mind and spirit on his dream, to write a book about the psychology of the concentration camp. Though he was nurtured by Freud, Frenkle

---

[27] Twenty-five mystical books written in the land of Israel, mostly referred to Jewish sages from the Talmudic time until the early Middle Ages.

rebelled against the notion that man lives to satisfy the will for pleasure. His entire theory of Logotherapy[28] claims that the deep finding of meaning is the key for surviving almost every challenge.

The search for meaning may cause suffering, but nobody was promised that life here would be fun. Purpose is definitely a key component in survival, and Jerusalem and the Holy Land gave the Jews exactly that. A symbol and a meaning, a belief in something far away that one day will make the suffering worth it. Because when it comes to us Jews, any Jew can tell you, suffering is the name of the game.

I don't claim to know how to answer Mark Twain's big philosophical question regarding the Jews and their survival. I do know that in my own search for connection and meaning, I believe I found the root for the survival of my people in the ancient Necropolis of Beit She'arim, and that is definitely something to write home about.

Menorah and sarcophagus, Beit She'arim[29]

---

[28] Based on the Greek word 'Logos' which translates to 'meaning'.

[29] Illustration: Dillon Krueger

CHASTELLET OF
JACOB'S FORD

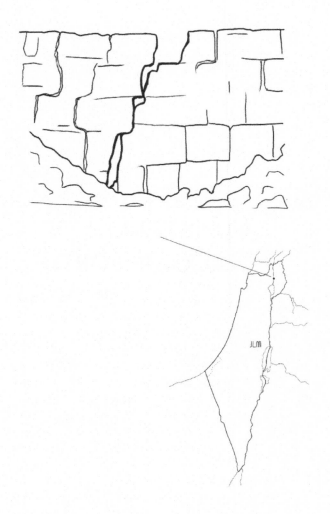

Chastellet of Jacob's Ford

Whenever I drive up to the Golan Heights, I always try to leave myself a little time to visit it. My favorite crack. Off of Route 91 there is a small dirt road that's very easy to miss. The road climbs up from the Hula Valley towards the Golan. It is scenic, steep and serpentine. Right in the middle of a steep, sharp curve, I make sure to drive real slow to break the steering wheel off road and park my car between the trees. Then I walk towards the massive limestone remains of the Crusaders' fortress, and I see it looking back at me in all its glory. The crack that marks the epic breaking point between east and west.

The entrance to the burial caves.[1]

---

[1] Source: Public Domain. (n.d.). Credit: Asaf Tz.

***

The first kingdom of Jerusalem was standing for 80 years when the terrible massacre took place here in 1179. The first decades of the kingdom were filled with war and the investment needed to construct a kingdom from scratch. When the crusaders first arrived in 1099 AD, they fought the Fatimid Caliphate and managed to establish an impressive kingdom.

Many of the known narratives about the crusaders are focused on the inner-European politics and the intrigues of the court. The regional politics of the Muslim Middle East are often skipped upon or generalized in regards to crusaders' history, and I believe that's a shame. The crusaders' point of view of themselves may have been eccentric, but in reality, the geopolitics in the Muslim side had a great influence on the crusaders' episode in the Holy Land, whether they knew it or not.

In a nutshell, the crusaders stood out like a sore thumb in the heart of the Muslim Middle East. An autonomist Christian presence wasn't seen in the land since the fall of the Byzantine in 638 AD. Since then, the land of Israel was under what is known today as "The Early Muslim Period," a name which doesn't do justice, in my humble opinion, with the number of caliphates, dynasties, tribes and independent rulers who fought over it and ruled it for several years or several decades at a time.

In this boiling cauldron of Muslim strife, the crusaders managed to achieve impressive results on the ground. Their kingdom stood as a barrier between the Suni Seljuk rule in Syria and the Shiite Fatimid rule in Egypt. Their superiority in battle was apparent, and they brought fighting techniques, methods, and abilities the Muslims had never encountered. For a while, the first Kingdom of Jerusalem did well in its conquests of the east and established a relatively stable entity in the land. However, it was in the crusaders' fortress called Chastellet, above the strategic point of Jacob's Ford, where their luck began to turn.

The Muslim reality the crusaders knew when they arrived at the Holy Land changed dramatically over eighty years of being a kingdom. The Muslims they met and fought against upon their arrival were divided, fractured into factions, and fought each other often. Within decades of its establishment though, the Christian Kingdom of Jerusalem became an enemy for the surrounding Muslim forces to unite against, and helped create the entity that would eventually bring its destruction.

The Seljuk dynasty in the north was led by Nur ad-Din, a Suni Muslim leader whose goal was to unite the different Muslim dynasties in the region under one dominion, and create a strong and united Seljuk Empire under his rule. For a while, his efforts were successful. By 1149, he had managed to unite Syria with Mosul (north Iraq), and his next step was taking down the Christian Kingdom of Jerusalem that stood between him and an uninterrupted empire, including the land of Israel and Fatimid Egypt. Alas, Nur ad-Din wasn't the only one with big dreams.

Ten years before the massacre done here in 1169, the crusaders under the rule of King Amalric I, took advantage of the political instability in Egypt and attempted to conquer it. Nur ad-Din sent his forces from Syria to Egypt, forced the crusaders back into their old territory, and nominated a ruler on his behalf by the name of Saladin.

Nur ad-Din went back to Syria, certain that Saladin, his former protege, would function as his loyal servant. Together, he thought, they could attack the crusaders' kingdom from the north and the south, defeat them, and establish a united Seljuk dynasty under Nur ad-Din's rule. Saladin also had plans to establish a Muslim territory between Syria and Egypt, but his plans didn't include Nur ad-Din.

While Nur ad-Din tried to initiate joint attacks against the crusaders, in which Nur ad-Din attacked from north-east and Saladin attacked from south-west in a wide 'pincer-move,' Saladin refused to take part in most of these attacks, and when he did take part in them, he made sure to not defeat the crusaders. Their presence between his territory in Egypt and Nur ad-Din's in Syria was a temporary interest of his. Instead of establishing a united Arab force that could defeat the crusaders, Nur-ad-Din created a new and powerful enemy.

While Saladin avoided battles or lost 'on purpose,' the crusaders earned more victories over the Saracens[2] to their record, gaining more confidence in their ability to stand against the Muslim enemy.

A war between Nur ad-Din and Saladin seemed inevitable, but never happened. Instead, Nur ad-Din died of fever in 1174. While his young son succeeded him, it didn't take long before Saladin marched to Syria, and in place of the Seljuk sultanate, established his own - the Ayyubid dynasty.

The new dynasty posed a threat that the crusaders never had to face before - a Saracen force united under one leader. The internal intrigues no longer stood between the Muslims and them, and Saladin's Ayyubid dynasty was getting ready to direct all of its might toward a Jihad[3] that would defeat the Crusaders once and for all.

---

[2] The European name for the Arabs in the time of the crusades.

[3] A Muslim holy war against the infidels

Meanwhile, back in Jerusalem, much happened. The king of Jerusalem, Amalric I, who was known for his bravery and an impressive record of triumphs against the Saracens, also died in 1174. Despite his son and heir Baldwin IV being a bright and capable young man, though he was merely thirteen years old, his coronation was bound to bring an era of instability to the kingdom, for despite his many virtues, Baldwin IV was a leper.

William of Tyre discovers Baldwin's first symptoms of leprosy, 1250.[4]

The disease attacked Baldwin IV when he was a child, and it had crucial implications for his reign. A leper was prevented from marrying and producing heirs. Under these conditions, the multicultural kingdom, with its old and new noblemen and with the less and less abiding knights-orders, became a concoction of schemes.

After establishing his rule over Syria and Egypt, it wasn't long until Saladin and Baldwin IV met in battle, in 1177. The battle took a heavy toll on both sides. After it, a cease-fire agreement was made, and each leader tended to his own camp.

Baldwin IV's first task was to barricade and fortify Jerusalem and the rest of the kingdom's settlements that were damaged during

---

[4] Source: France, 1250. The British Library of London, Public Domain.

the war. Inside his kingdom though, the tension was rising. Baldwin IV may have been king, but not all of the crusaders in Jerusalem were subordinate to the king. The order of the Knights Templar and the order of the Knights Hospitaller were subordinate directly to the Pope. While they were of great help to the kingdom as a standing army, they were often aggressive and blood-thirsty and hawkish in their approach. Baldwin IV often found himself having to bend to their will to keep them at his side, which is exactly what happened in the fortress of Jacob's Ford.

The name 'Jacob's Ford' was assigned to this place by the crusaders, who mistook it for being the ford of the Jabbok:

> *"That night Jacob got up and took his two wives, his two female servants and his eleven sons and crossed the ford of the Jabbok."*
>
> -   *Genesis 32:22 (NIV)*

Jacob's Ford was the only crossing point of the Jordan River between its sources and the Dead Sea. In order to travel between Syria and Egypt, crossing this point is inevitable, which made it a high-value target for Saladin, who had to cross it in order to connect between his two centers of rule. Furthermore, the road passing through there was used by Muslim pilgrims. During the first decades of fighting between the Saracens and the Crusaders, a few acts of war were off limits - never hurt trade convoys, never hurt pilgrims, never contaminate the water sources.

Despite the high sensitivity of the location, or perhaps because of it, the Knights Templar pressured Baldwin IV to build a fort to guard it, as a strategic move. Baldwin IV wasn't a fan of the idea at first, but due to the delicate situation in his court, he agreed and in 1179, the work of building the new fort began.

Example for a fort within a fort: Krak des Chevaliers, Middle Ages.[5]

The fort was named "Chastellet" in French, which meant "The Little Fort"[6], and it was designed to be a "concentric fort"[7]. A concentric fort was one of the Crusaders' most magnificent and sophisticated structures, for it meant "a fort within a fort". Double the walls, double the gates, double the towers. Though it was designed to be a relatively small fortress, the fortifications were meant to be massive.

The construction of this fortress on such a strategic point, was like sticking a finger in Saladin's eye. Nonetheless, Saladin decided to take the diplomatic approach, and sent an offer to Baldwin IV. The offer stated that though Saladin considered the building of the fort to be a violation of their truce, he was willing to pay a sum of 60,000 golden coins, to compensate for the cost of the building, and halt construction.

---

[5] Source: Public Domain. Credit: Guillaume Rey.
[6] Ellenblum, R. Marco, S. Agnon, A. Rockwell, T. Boas, A. (1998). *Crusaders Castle Torn Apart by Earthquake at Dawn*, 20 May 1202. Hebrew University. Jerusalem. Pp. 1-4.

[7] Boas, A. (1999). *Crusader archaeology: the material culture of the Latin East*. Routledge. Pp. 115

Despite the diplomatic offer, Baldwin refused. Surprisingly, a second offer soon arrived. This time, Saladin offered a sum of one hundred thousand gold coins. This extremely generous offer was also declined by the crusader's king.

Saladin's diplomatic attempts may have failed, but his goal hadn't changed. A crusaders' fortress couldn't be built to control this crossing point, and he knew very well that in order to take it down, he must act quickly. Once the fort was finished, it would be almost impenetrable. The Europeans were great builders, so he knew, and as long as they kept barricading in their forts, they were out of reach.

This fortress was still in progress, and bringing it down was still possible. According to Latin and Muslim sources, the fort was rectangular, and made of twenty thousand bricks that were each seven feet long. The external wall didn't exist yet, nor did the complex gateway. One tower stood, while the rest were still under construction. The time to attack was now[8].

On August 24th, 1179, the attack began. Saladin opened a siege and told his troops to attack simultaneously from the east and the west. His plan was to dig a tunnel that would reach underneath the fortress wall, then burn the beams supporting it, causing a segment of the wall to collapse. To cover the sappers and their helpers, Saladin's archers were constantly shooting arrows from a distance of over two hundred yards into the fortress.

The Crusaders understood that Saladin was attempting to bring down their wall, and their archers were shooting at the sappers and anyone who made his way into the tunnel.

---

[8] Hebrew University of Jerusalem. (2007). *Vadum Iacob Research Project. The Templar Castle of Vadum Iacob - "Jacob's Ford"*. Official Website.

The first attempt to set fire underground failed. The fire was burning in the tunnel but the walls weren't damaged. If I had to guess, I'd say that at this point, Saladin was probably sweating, and not necessarily due to the August weather. It wouldn't be long before Baldwin IV arrived with back up to save his men in Chastellet. Saladin didn't want to fight Baldwin IV, he wanted to send him a message.

The fire kept burning in the tunnel and Saladin knew he wasn't going to get a second attempt until it would fade. The immediate solution would be to send his soldiers to fetch water from the Jordan River, which was merely five hundred meters away, but the crusaders' archers were aiming and hitting anyone who made his way to the river.

"One golden Dinar for anyone who brings a bucket of water from the river!" Saladin finally declared, and his men embraced the task, and the reward, and managed to put out the fire.

The second attempt was successful. The sappers dug all the way to the beams and set them on fire. On August 30th, 1179, the wall collapsed, and the Saracens stormed Chastellet.

The battle was brutal. Saladin's forces set fire to the castle and its surroundings. According to Latin and Muslim sources, when the commander of the knights saw the wall falling and the Muslim soldiers storming the castle, in his despair, he made his horse jump off the tower, and dove with it into the blazing fire, dying in just moments.

The crusaders begged for a cease-fire, but Saladin refused. As his forces advanced further into the castle, the crusaders' garrisons were pushed further and further inward until they were backed into the main gate.

When the battle was done, the castle was ablaze. The survivors begged for mercy. Saladin was known for his clemency, but this time was different. Out of one thousand, five hundred men who were found in the castle, eight hundred died in combat or were butchered by Saladin. The archers were executed first. The rest, about seven hundred people, were taken captive. Afterwards, he commanded his soldiers to raze the castle to the ground.

To ensure that the Crusaders will never try to establish their dominance over the crossing point, Saladin then ordered to fill the water well with the bodies of the dead. This act contaminated the drinking water for long long after, assuring no one will return or try and take control over it for many years to come.

Saladin's message was heard loud and clear. Baldwin IV didn't just "lose a piece off the board". The knights who were killed in Chastellet were people he was familiar with and though he rode from Tiberias to their rescue, he didn't make it in time. The massacre of Jacob's Ford was written in historical records as his first loss.

From then on, the balance of power was decided. Though it took ten more years and Baldwin IV's death for Saladin to defeat the crusaders and erase the first Kingdom of Jerusalem off the map, the battle of Jacob's Ford was a turning point. From this battle and on, Saladin began to win. Thought the wars between the Franks[9] and the Saracens didn't stop, and while Baldwin IV did manage to gain some impressive achievements on the battlefield, the defeat at Chastellet marked the beginning of the end for the first Kingdom of Jerusalem.

---

[9] A nickname for the Crusaders

Saladin The Vicrorious, Gustave Doré, 19ᵗʰ Century. [10]

***

The crusaders left Israel with what can be called the most impressive archeological era in the land. Fortified castles standing whole, churches that still stand and function today, and countless

---

[10] Source: Public Domain. Credit: Gustave Doré, 19ᵗʰ Century.

written sources to compare the findings to, all carrying the delicious scent of thousand-year-old history.

Excavating a crusaders' fortress is quite the exciting mission. To start, the structures are so well constructed, most of them still stand almost whole today. Second, the materialistic culture was very developed and highly documented, which makes for a higher likelihood for plentiful findings. Third, the Kingdoms of Jerusalem were very well-documented by the Crusaders themselves, by Europe who had many connections with it, and by the Muslim historians of Saladin.

For archeologists however, there are three more elements that can make a Crusaders archeological site even better - a war that caused destruction, a short time of use which narrows down verifying the dating of the findings, and a permanent desertion of the site with no secondary use. Chastellet, to the great joy of the archeologists, includes all three.

From construction to destruction, the castle was active and populated for ten to eleven months. While Saladin took apart the fortress and not much of it is left to see except a few foundational walls, for archeologists, this place was like a feast. After the battle, the fortress was deserted, likely due to the contamination of the water source, and the destruction and chaos of war kept it "as is," covered only by the dust of time.

This made the excavations done here since 1994 by the Hebrew University of Jerusalem that much more exciting. The excavation revealed the awful massacre that happened there and made the eighth-hundred-year-old atrocities that much more vivid.

More than one thousand, two hundred arrowheads were found in what was only 15% of the area that needed excavation. This is a small portion of the number of arrows that were probably shot, given that a skilled archer was able to shoot about twelve arrows per minute. The skeletons that were revealed in the castle and around it were found with their limbs randomly positioned, and none were given a proper burial.

Close to the wall, a skeleton of a warrior was found in the exact place and physical position in which he died, with a 200kg rock on his chest. The rock was probably dropped on him from the top of the wall by the defenders of Châstellet.

Another warrior's skeleton was found with a treasure still in his grasp. A fabric sack, that at this point was dissolved to be nothing but several crumbling threads, with a treasure of one hundred and sixty silver coins, printed with the image of Amalric I on one side, and the church of Holy Sepulcher on the other. This small and personal treasure, fits perfectly to the time of the massacre, and is a rare finding that can help us learn much about the kingdom's economic structure.

Among the skeletons were different Equidae, such as horses, mules and donkeys, all taking part in the defense. Many of the horses were shot, often by arrows designed for killing beasts, as they were a large target to aim at, and harder to defend and protect. However, even the archeologists who are used to revealing the horrors of war, were in awe of this next finding. As part of the massacre and the general destruction, pigs, who were bred for meat and were an integral part of the crusaders' diet, were deliberately executed. Instead of being slaughtered, they were shot and left to rot. Since pigs are considered impure in Islam and are forbidden as food, the pigs who dwelled in Chastellet were also victims of the massacre (though I suppose that the only difference for said pigs was that they didn't end up on a plate post mortem). As they say in French - "*a la guerre comme a la guerre*" - in war as in war, even the bacon wasn't spared.

**

Now, it is time for a small confession. There are far more impressive crusaders' sites in Israel. Castles standing whole and original fortifications that can be used to shoot the next Middle Age Hollywood movie. Next to those, Chastellet is nothing to write home about. Any tour guide or tourist knows that the recipe for a good tour site must contain a good story, along with something extremely impressive to look at. To be honest, while Chastellet is an archeologist's dream, and while it has an excellent war story of great significance to crusader history, the site itself can be disappointing for anyone who doesn't know where to look.

When arriving at Chastellet, an ordinary-looking wall welcomes visitors. The wall is about twenty meters (sixty-five feet) long, and is made of large hewn limestone bricks, filled with roughly carved basalt stones. Behind the wall are the rest of the remains of the fort, but on 90% of my visits, I never bothered to go look at them. Instead, I make my way to a very unusual crack in the left side of the wall.

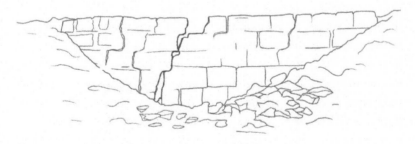

A very unusual crack in the wall [11]

The crack is vertical and parts the wall as if part of it moved forward and the other part stayed behind. It looks almost as if a giant played with the castle like it was a toy, and carelessly just… gave it a little pinch and pushed part of it slightly forward. The

---

[11] Illustration: Dillon Krueger.

castle remained standing, so it's almost like 'no harm was done.' Not every person has a favorite crack, but I do. Out of all the cracks I've encountered in my professional life, this one is by far, my favorite. Among my many sins, I have always had a strong affection for things that are unique. To the best of my knowledge, this crack is one of a kind not only in Israel, but in the world. At least for now.

When Baldwin IV ordered the construction of the castle, he had no way to know that this specific location was right on a seam line between two tectonic plates. The crack in the front wall was created by the movement of the plates.

The active geological fault tore the castle apart from south to north[12], which meant that the Eastern part of the fort is on the Arab Plate, while the Western part of the fort is on the African Plate. In other words, geologically speaking, the fort is half in Asia, and half in Africa[13].

The history of the land of Israel is tremendously influenced by its location and by geology. A short glimpse at the world's map reveals that while Africa and Asia are completely separate continents, Africa is "hanging by a thread" on the Asian-European bloc, and that

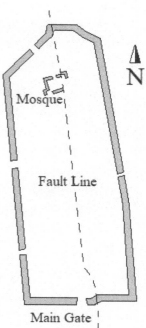

---

[12] Ellenblum, R. Marco, S. Agnon, A. Rockwell, T. Boas, A. (1998). *Crusaders Castle Torn Apart by Earthquake at Dawn*, 20 May 1202. Hebrew University. Jerusalem. Pp. 1

[13] Illustration: Public Domain. Credit: Asaf Tz. 2006.

thread is the land of Israel. This made Israel the only land route connecting Africa to Asia and Europe. There was no other way.

Anyone, be he a merchant carrying goods, a general in the head of an army, a pilgrim heading to a holy site, or a king on a campaign, needed this route to complete their intercontinental quests. From the Pharaohs of Egypt to Alexander the Great, from the Roman Empire to the Crusaders, from Saladin to the Ottoman Empire and from Napoleon Bonaparte to the British Empire, it was clear: the key to building an intercontinental empire lies in the land of Israel.

The geological separation between the continents of Asia and Africa, is an active fault known as the DST - the Dead Sea Transform. This fault transfers opening at the Red Sea and the Gulf of Aden to the collision between Arabia and Eurasia along the Taurus-Zagros Mountain belt.

Inside the current borders of Israel, the fault creates a long and relatively narrow valley from the Galilee in the north, through the Dead Sea[14] in the middle, and all the way to the Red Sea in the south. From the mountains of the upper Galilee, down to the Sea of Galilee and from the Sea of Galilee south to the Dead Sea, is the route of the Biblical Jordan River. From the south part of the Sea of Galilee and down to the Red Sea, the valley also marks the current border between the State of Israel and the Kingdom of Jordan.

The Dead Sea Transform is still active, which implies that the continents are still in the process of separating. This fact is manifested into the history of the land of Israel by a long list of powerful and destructive earthquakes. On average, every ninety to one hundred and twenty years, a massive earthquake strikes, causing destruction and carnage. The last massive earthquake was

---

[14] The Dead Sea became the lowest place on earth precisely due to said fault.

in 1927, so if you're thinking about moving to Israel, I'd give it a few more years.

The crusaders never experienced an earthquake in Chastellet, given that it was populated for less than a year. However, the ruins of it remained standing for almost eight hundred and fifty years, surviving not one but two massive earthquakes. One occurred in 1202, and the other in 1759. The exact location of the castle on the seam line of the DST fault, combined with the Crusaders' superb construction abilities, caused it to tear apart, rather than fall apart.

Shakked, examining the crack, 2018.

The geologist Amotz Agnon[15] conducted thorough research on Chastellet, and measured a total movement of 2.1 meters altogether. However, on top of one of the ruined towers, a small mosque was built, probably around the late Mamluk period, and used during the time of the Ottoman Empire. The mosque was also torn apart, but only by 0.5 meters. This led to the conclusion that the earthquake of May 1202 caused a movement of 1.6 meters, while the earthquake of 1759 caused the additional 0.5 meters. So, why is it important?

---

[15] Grandson of the Nobel Prize laureate writer Shmuel Yosef Agnon.

Despite many large earthquakes known to have occurred in the Middle East throughout history, neither caused surface ruptures, nor have displacements of man-made structures by fault-slip been recorded until the archaeological excavations of Chastellet.

This finding provides the ability to date the earthquake with maximal accuracy, and estimate its intensity. It also helps scientists calculate the amount of energy accumulating in the earth's crust, thus better predicting the frequency and intensity of future earthquakes in the area. This is the first time in history that the study of an archeological site is vital and greatly contributes to the study of the seismology of major earthquakes.

Chastellet, or "Ateret"[16] in its Hebrew name, can easily be classified, superficially speaking, as one of the least impressive sites in Israel. Nonetheless, sometimes it's the places nobody imagines anything of, that conceal the things no one can imagine[17]. I may be crazy, but when I look at this crack, I see the essence of the land of Israel, as a bridge of cultures and a discord point of faiths. A single crack in the wall of a single ruined fortress symbolizes so many things. A geological meeting point between Africa and Eurasia, a historical clashing point between Eastern and Western culture, between Islam and Christianity, a place where the ground shakes with anger, but the walls still stand.

Not too bad for a crack, huh?

---

[16] The Muslims used to call this place "Qasr al Athra", which means "The Fortress of Failure". The name penetrated into the Hebrew language and was converted phonetically to "Ateret", which means "crown" or "tiara".

[17] Borrowed from the quote by Alan Turing: *"Sometimes it's the people who no one imagines anything of, that do things no one can imagine"*.

SECRET ISRAEL

GILGAL REPHAIM
WHEEL OF THE NEPHILIM

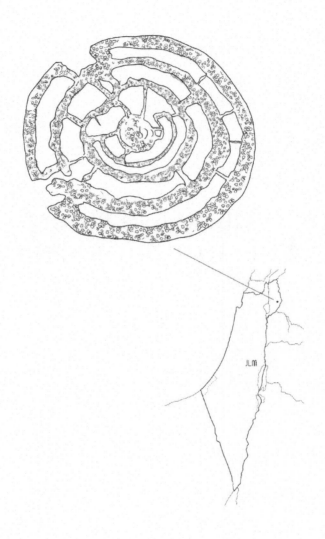

Gilgal Rephaim
Wheel of the Nephilim

I am deeply troubled by this particular site, and I am not going to sugar coat why. There is a site in Israel that is shaped like a circle, in which every question asked, is replied not with an answer, but with another question. An endless loop.

Gilgal Rephaim is a site in Israel that nobody knows how to explain. It is a five-thousand-year-old megalithic structure of concentric circles, with a chamber in its center. Throughout history, no one knew it was there because it is too widespread to be seen from the ground, so it wasn't until someone flew over it in 1969 that it was discovered. For over fifty years, scholars have been studying it and trying to make sense of it, but none could find a definitive answer as to what this place is, or who built it. Thorough interdisciplinary research found fragments of information that might make sense separately, but none of them can be put together to create a full picture of this circle shaped puzzle.

A warning to science-oriented readers. While the rest of the sites in this book are anchored by facts, scriptures and research, even those in which the storytelling element is more dominant, this chapter is a bit of a stretch. There is a lot of information out there about the different elements that make up this site, and as much fun as it is to intellectually play with exciting guesses and ideas, this chapter is the only one in this book where I am not clinging to facts and scientific thinking, and jumping into the abstract and occasionally supernatural world of philosophy, mythology, and etymology.

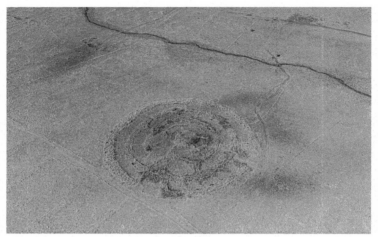

Gilgal Rephaim from the air, 2020[1]

The readers of this chapter are about to join me on a journey outside of my comfort zone. Consider yourselves warned.

The other option, in the face of the challenges this site poses, would be to lose this chapter altogether, but the stories concerning it are simply too good, and my adventurous conscience won't allow it.

The usual spine of a site will always be the chronology, but with Gilgal Rephaim there is hardly any. The site was built by an unidentified nation, approximately five thousand years ago, sometime between the late Chalcolithic and Early Bronze era, and that's about it. It was soon deserted, and then disappeared, completely absent from the pages of history until it was

---

[1] Source: Pikiwiki photo stock. Credit: Chaim Shafir, drone shot, 2020.

discovered again by an Israeli aircraft pilot in 1969, shortly after the Six-Day War. The pilot reported noticing an odd-looking circular structure while flying over the Golan Heights. Soon enough, photos were taken and the research began.

Indeed, Gilgal Rephaim is first and foremost intriguing, considering that while the circles in it are precise and seem extremely impressive, no one can see them just by standing on the ground. From the ground, Gilgal Rephaim looks like nothing more than a heap of stones, which probably gave it the name it was known by on old Syrian maps: 'Rujum El Hiri', simply translated into "The Stone Pile of the Wild Cat." The name of it is meaningless, as it is a very late one, given by people who haven't used the place, nor knew what it stood for. It is only from a considerable height that you can fully appreciate the geometric wonder this place reveals itself to be.

The matter gets even more complicated, considering the flat landscape Gilgal Rephaim was built upon. The glory of this megalithic structure can only be fully appreciated from above, from a significantly higher point of view. Nonetheless, there are no mountains or hills anywhere around from which the structure can be seen.

Many important questions are raised in the study of this place. For instance, what sort of culture, ruler or nation, would build a megalithic structure they can never fully see or appreciate? Not to mention that it required so many resources and meticulous planning and work to build. Who were these people? What happened to them? What did they use this structure for? And most importantly, how come there is no other structure similar to this one anywhere in the Middle East? How can it be that the closest circular structure of this sort and from this era is in India? All of these questions, along with the wild answers, suggested by different experts, make the study of this place surreal, and we haven't even scratched the surface.

Shmarya Guttman was the archeologist in charge of excavating this site, hoping to unveil its secrets, but due to no fault of his own, the study of Gilgal Rephaim didn't reveal much at all. It provided but dry details. These may be a bit of a 'technical read,' but they are essential for understanding how mind-blowing the site really is.

The structure is a round megalithic monument made of local unhewn basalt rocks in the shape of five concentric circles. Some of the circles are open and some are closed, which makes it into more of a spiral. The original height of the circles' walls was probably around five meters high, but today they aren't higher than two and a half meters at the most. The diameter of the external circle is one hundred, fifty-six meters and the length of it is five hundred meters, with two clearly ceremonial entrances.[2]. All of this makes the structure into the largest megalithic monument in the region, placing it in the same "pantheon" as places like the Pyramids, Stonehenge and others.

Fascinatingly enough, megalithic construction is observed in different centers of civilization around the ancient world in approximately the same timeframe. This fact is shocking, given that to the best of our knowledge today, there were no connections between these societies, and yet, they seem to have developed on a parallel axis[3].

---

[2] Marcus, M. (2001). *The New Israel Guide*. Volume 2. Hermon, Golan, and the Hula Valley. Keter Publishing House. Jerusalem. Pp. 104-105.

[3] Kamar, A. (2016). *Gilgal Rephaim - The Mysterious Site in the Golan Heights*. Ecology & Science. Ynet.

The structure is made out of approximately forty-two thousand basalt stones, and the construction gets more and more dense the closer it is to the center. In the center is a twenty-meter-wide dolmen, rising to the slightly more impressive height of about five meters, and in its belly, there is a chamber. The chamber is roofed with rocks that weigh a few tons each. In my eyes, the thought about such ancient cultures managing to lift rocks of this weight is impressive.

What is this structure? What was the use of it? And why is it in the shape of a circle? Many suggestions were made to guess the function of Gilgal Rephaim, all may be plausible, but none are satisfying, or answer all the questions put together. To be true to the scholar within me, I will attempt to present the different suggestions brought by different experts in the field. After that however, we shall take a leap into the world of mythology, supernatural, and wild assumptions, with low probability and no solid base.

The first and most popular suggestion is that Gilgal Rephaim is a burial site. This assumption is both correct and incorrect at the same time. In the middle chamber, archeologists revealed a burial site, and though no human remains were found, some artifacts like beads, jewelry and arrowheads could indicate that it was indeed used for burial. Unfortunately, further study determined that the burial section was only used one thousand years after the site was already built, and used for something else.

Others claim that this structure is a "Dakhma," also known as a "Tower of Silence," a Zoroastrian structure used for their unique method of burial. Zoroastrianism originated in Persia and considers the dead to be impure. A Dakhma is a burial structure made of concentric circles, on top of which the dead bodies are laid to be eaten and devoured by vultures. The male bodies are traditionally placed on the external circle, the females on the second, and the children on the innermost one. Only after six months, when the bones have been dried and "purified" by the sun, can the bones be placed in the ground. The closeness of Persia to the region and the circular shape of the structure would suggest that this could very well be a Dakhma, but unfortunately, the theory is flawed. While Zoroastrianism appeared in the beginning of the first thousand BC, Gilgal Rephaim stood in all its glory at least two thousand years before that. The absence of human remains is also a major flaw in the theory, not to mention the distance, considering that the closest Dakhma is found in Iran.

Iranian Tower of Silence, Early 20th Century. [4]

So perhaps it is not a Dakhma.

Some scholars claim that Gilgal Rephaim was used as a center of worship or religious ritual. Which religious ritual they mean is not quite clear. The basis for this assumption is a single window with

[4] Source: Public Domain. Credit: Project Gutenberg Literary Archive Foundation.

a very unique attribute in the central chamber. This is the only window in the entire central structure, and archeologists discovered that it was built at a shockingly calculated angle as well as with a very accurate measurement of the thickness of the wall. Through this window, the sunbeams can only penetrate the chamber on the solstice, the longest day of the year. On this day, the earth achieves its maximum axial tilt, allowing the sun to cast its rays through the window and into the chamber. These are incredible calculations for such an early era in history. Though this particular sun beam doesn't shed much light on the purpose of this structure, it does help us realize how sophisticated and knowledgeable the ancient nations that dwelled here were.

The angle of the sunbeam through the window made other scholars suggest that this structure may have been a facility for astronomical measurements and calculations. While it is an interesting thought, no astronomers nor meteorologists were able to point out the advantage or function this structure would provide in its unique form or location.

Thus, the mystery of this wheel remains standing. No hints, no clues, no answers. On a personal level, writing about this place threw me for a serious loop. It almost feels like a spiritual journey inside a circle, that doesn't begin or end anywhere. There is no logic, order, or sense of direction.

When you lose your orientation, the best thing to do is to find a compass and look for the north. Interestingly enough, Gilgal Rephaim is made of gigantic concentric circles, with two straight lines crossing through it. One points towards the rising sun in the east, and the other points towards the highest mountain in Israel, in the north. So that might be a good place to start.

The highest mountain of a region was often considered in ancient cultures as the 'axis mundi,' the axle of the world. The construction of a megalithic structure that points towards the sun on one hand and the axis mundi on the other could be an attempt to achieve some sort of harmony.

A psychological attempt to explain Gilgal Rephaim from a Jungian and almost mystical point of view, claims that the ancient world didn't separate between burial, ritual and study. The burial place of the ancient ancestors would be considered a temple and a source of wisdom[5]. According to this approach, the circular construction appears in different tribal cultures as a primeval, mentally imprinted shape, like a mandala, and the purpose of it is to restore harmony that was lost.

The intent behind such a structure could be an attempt of the unknown people who dwelled near it, to appease the higher forces threatening to diminish them. This theory is fascinating, considering Gilgal Rephaim's unique location and time of construction. The Golan heights is a magmatic turf. While most of the magmatic activity stopped one hundred thousand years ago, beyond the current state borders between Israel and Syria, in the currently Syrian Golan, there is magmatic activity that's only a few thousand years old. Perhaps the people of Gilgal Rephaim witnessed the soil spitting fire and tried to take responsibility and restore order in the world?

As promised, more questions than answers. After we've paid our debt to science, it is time to dive deep, into the origin of the name Gilgal Rephaim, and to introduce the mythological and Biblical nations who dwelled in this region. It is time to meet the giants.

***

---

[5] Ankori, M. (2020). *Rujum El Hiri - The Riddle of Unity*. Online Lecture by Dr. Micha Ankori.

Og the Giant

Old Og was laying in his giant bed and felt lonelier than ever. The war was almost at his door. He could feel it, and there wasn't much he could do. A few days ago, a few Emorites arrived at night and reported the murder of their king, Sihon. The Hebrews of the desert made their way along the valley, and they intended to cross the Jordan and take over the land. Should they choose to cross above the Dead Sea, so the surviving Emorites thought, maybe they would never make it to the Bashan, and safety would be guaranteed.

Og's instinct told him otherwise.

He'd been waiting for it for years, and it's finally here. His last battle. His heart filled with sadness.

"The Israelites are coming, my king," the head of spies came back and told him last night. "They are moving every day and by tomorrow, they will be at the verge of Bashan[6]. Their camp is huge, more than the eye could see. Women and children were at the camp too, but the young men were plenty, and strong. Desert-born folk with one goal - to conquer the land of Israel."

'The desert has come to take me,' Og thought. 'How fitting.'

Being the last of his kind, his life felt like a desert already. It had been years since he had spoken to a fellow giant. What was once a great nation had dissolved until all that was left was one lonely and heavy-hearted king, who felt excluded and out of date. Og was tired. He didn't want to fight, nor did he want to admit that the end was finally here. Not just for him, but for what once was a glorious dynasty of his proud and fierce ancestors. It was for them, and

---

[6] Biblical name for the Golan.

only for them, that he found it within himself to leave his comfy bed and start preparing his kingdom for war.

Old Og was the last of the Rephaites, a nation of giants who ruled the Bashan. Once, they were known as great and fearless warriors who intimidated nations just by appearing at their gates. Legends and superstitions were tied to their names. Some said they had supernatural powers, others suggested that they could communicate with spirits, and some even said that the Rephaites were demonic angels of the underworld. It was all nonsense, Og knew, but there was no silencing the wicked tongues, and while the Rephaites were great warriors, they despised the attention and the nosy humans who stared at them with their eyes wide open, whispering Gods know what to one another. To avoid the unwelcome attention, they set their kingdom in the Bashan, a good flat herding land, yet up on the heights, overlooking the Sea of Galilee, far from the realms of men. The Bashan for them was a kingdom of refuge. It was a haven, where they could live their lives uninterrupted. No one dared attack the uplifted kingdom of the giant Rephaites.

Back when Og was just a child, he remembered sitting on his grandpa's lap, listening to his tales. His grandpa told him how the giant Rephaites were the descendants of the great 'Nephilim.' When little Og asked who the Nephilim were, his grandpa smiled and simply told him he's too young to understand these kinds of things. He did tell him that the Nephilim were great entities on earth, so great that they managed to survive the great flood and live among humans. Og smiled a sad smile. Even old giants missed their grandfathers sometimes.

Slowly, Og dragged his cracking joints to the old chest, pulled out his old, dusty battle suite, and laid it on his bed. He hadn't had a good fight in years, he thought. He looked at the enormous spear leaning against the wall and walked down to the big lake to wash up. The cool water made him feel fresh again. His reflection stared back at him from the water. 'The last of the Rephaites,' he thought sadly of the great people they were. All the glorious fighters who because of their physical advantage survived the flood, but not the test of time. He realized that while the lonely and drained old giant in him wanted nothing more than to lay in bed and die in peace, another voice, an ancient and profound entity imprinted deep inside of him, knew that giants don't die in their beds. 'If we are destined to perish,' Og said back to his reflection in the water, 'Rephaites go down fighting.'

***

The story of Og always made me sad. I know, I know, I am descended from the Israelites, and if it weren't for them I probably wouldn't be here, blah blah blah… But the thought of Og being the last of his fellow giants and then getting killed in battle alongside his sons still breaks my heart a little.

Goliath the Giant by Osmar Schindler. 1888.
Goliagh was descendant of Rapha, 1 Chronicles 20:8. [7]

---

[7] Source: Public Domain. Credit: Osmar Schindler.

The name Gilgal Rephaim is rather new. It was given to this site as a substitute to its Syrian name. The word "Gilgal" means "Wheel", and the word "Rephaim" stands for the ancient Rephaites, the giants who dwelled in the area. For me however, despite being a Hebrew speaker, the name "Rephaites" or more correctly "Rephaim" to mean ancient giants, was a big surprise. The word Rephaim in current spoken Hebrew doesn't refer to the ancient Rephaites anymore, at least not commonly. It is used to describe ghosts or spirits.

This fact raised a few questions in my head. How come the name 'Rephaim' in phonetic Hebrew, or "Rephaites" in English, evolved from describing Biblical giants, to describing ghosts?

To further understand, I dove into the Bible in a quest to understand the giants.

It seems that giants are mentioned in the Torah a considerable number of times. The Rephaites are described as the descendants of Anak, and the Anakites were related to the Nephilim. When someone understands the complex nature of the Nephilim, the double meaning of the name Rephaim, is starting to make a slight, but just slight, sense.

> *"The Nephilim were on the earth in those days—and also afterward—when the sons of God went to the daughters of humans and had children by them. They were the heroes of old, men of renown."*
>
> - *Genesis 6:4 NIV*

This fascinating verse is one of the most ambiguous verses in the Bible. It appears as part of the stories of creation, and it is the last verse in the chapter before the story of Noah and the Flood begins. The interpreters of this verse are divided about whether the Nephilim were the children of the sons of God and the daughters of humans, or perhaps they already existed when those children were born. This debate is not as important for Gilgal Rephaim, mostly due to the fact that there is no definite answer and it is all open for interpretation, but what is important, is their relation in some manner, to a mythic occurrence in the process of creation.

The Fall of the Rebel Angels, Hieronymus Bosch, 16th Century. [8]

The Hebrew root of the name "Nephilim" is N.PH.L. which means "to fall," and their actual name means "those who have fallen" or even "those who have been dropped." A vague name for vague people. Right after, the verse mentions them as heroes, which is probably the stem for their description as an intimidating bunch as the story unfolds. So there we have it. Mythical people who were present before and after the flood, with a name that indicates that

---

[8] Source: Public Domain. Credit: Hieronymus Bosch, 1506-1518

there might be some chance that they came down from a divine territory into the human world. They might be the children of angels and human ladies, and also brave warriors. Now that's the substance for a good plot! I love the Bible.

The next mention of Nephilim occurred in the book of Numbers. The Israelites were at the borders of the promised land, and Moses is sending spies to explore and come back with a detailed report. When the spies return, they bring very disturbing news:

> *"But the people who live there are powerful, and the cities are fortified and very large. We even saw descendants of Anak there...The land we explored devours those living in it. All the people we saw there are of great size. We saw the Nephilim there (the descendants of Anak come from the Nephilim). We seemed like grasshoppers in our own eyes, and we looked the same to them."*
>
> - *Numbers 13:28-33 NIV*

So the Nephilim were dwelling in the promised land, or at the very least the spies identified them as Nephilim. They are described as large and powerful; some even interpret the verse to imply that they are feasting on human flash. They are also described as related to "Anak"[9]. This is the last mention of the Nephilim in the Bible. The next time the Israelites are meeting giants, they are no longer called Nephilim, but rather Rephaites, and they are also said to be related to Anak. From here we deduce that the Rephaites and the Nephilim are definitely related:

---

[9] "Anak" in current spoken Hebrew is commonly used as an adjective, to express "huge, giant, gigantic" etc.

"The Emites used to live there—a people strong and numerous, and as tall as the Anakites. Like the Anakites, they too were considered Rephaites, but the Moabites called them Emites."

- ***Deuteronomy 2:10-11 NIV***

Soon enough, the Israelites battled their way through the nations surrounding the promised land, and after going through Moab and killing Sihon the King of the Emorites, they arrived at the Bashan. 'Bashan' is the Biblical name for the Golan. The ruler of the Bashan is Og, who is described as the last of the Rephaites. In battle, the Israelites kill him and his sons, and make the land into their territory:

"The rest of Gilead and also all of Bashan, the kingdom of Og, I gave to the half-tribe of Manasseh. (The whole region of Argob in Bashan used to be known as a land of the Rephaites...Og king of Bashan was the last of the Rephaites. His bed was decorated with iron and was more than nine cubits long and four cubits wide."

- ***Deuteronomy 3:11-13 NIV***

"Then they turned and went up along the road toward Bashan, and Og king of Bashan and his whole army marched out to meet them in battle at Edrei. The Lord said to Moses, "Do not be afraid of him, for I have delivered him into your hands, along with his whole army and his land. Do to him what you did to Sihon king of the Amorites, who reigned in Heshbon." So they struck him down, together with his sons and his whole army, leaving them no survivors. And they took possession of his land."

- ***Numbers 21:33-35 NIV***

107

At this point, Og was killed and with him, the nation of the Rephaites[10].

Fascinatingly enough, the mentions of the Rephaites didn't stop, they just changed their context. In the various English translations for the Bible, every next mention of the word "Rephaim," is translated into 'spirits,' 'dead,' or 'deceased.' For a reason that isn't known to me, the use of the word 'Rephaites,' though completely identical in its spelling in Hebrew, isn't being used 'as is' in the English translations. From now on, the Rephaites are mentioned in regards to resurrection prophecies, and Hell, or Sheol:

> *The realm of the dead* (in Hebrew: Rephaim) *below is all astir to meet you at your coming; it rouses the spirits of the departed to greet you...*

> - *Isaiah 14:9 NIV*

> *But he knoweth not that the dead* (in Hebrew: Rephaim) *are there; and that her guests are in the depths of hell.*

> - *Proverbs 9:18 KJV*

The Rephaites, a nation of giants historically known for living in the Golan heights, is killed, but instead of dying, evolves into a world of spirits connected with the underworld. How does it all connect to our story of Gilgal Rephaim? I'm glad you asked. It doesn't, really. Not directly anyways. Considering no physical or empirical evidence was found for giants ever walking the land, again, to the best of my knowledge, we can't tie between this

---

[10] In 2 Samuel 21:19-22, Goliath the giant of Gath is mentioned once again, as one of the descended from Rapha. The verse doesn't explain much more, but this could be a hint that maybe not all the Rephaites were gone from the world.

Biblical nation and any historical site for that matter. Nonetheless, my creative head that tends to work extra hours, did find a few interesting links, at least intellectually speaking.

For starters, one of the astonishing elements about Gilgal Rephaim is that it cannot be seen in all its glory, unless watched from above. Furthermore, no mountains, hills or even natural forests are near this megalith, to fully enjoy it from. It is amusing to imagine a nation of giants supervising the construction of these perfectly concentric circles. Alright, alright, I suppose the builders could have used scaffolds. But it's still fun to think about.

Another overlap that I find great is the Hebrew root for Og's name. In Hebrew, for no apparent reason (I really did look), the letters making his name are the same lingual root stem for the word....

circle.

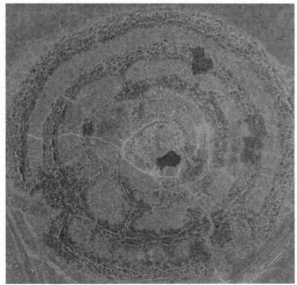

Gilgal Rephaim, satellite view, 2021.

Is there a connection between Og's name and the circular structure? We will probably never know.

To make things even better, another play on words is joining the game. Two meanings we've mentioned so far for the word "Rephaim" - ancient Biblical giants, and ghosts or spirit of the underworld. The root of this word however, R. PH. A., also stands for the Hebrew word for "healing." To sooth the wrath of Hebrew speaking scholars who must be boiling at the bold leaps I take with no parachute, a word of appeasement - the fact that I find something cool and fitting for the patterns in my head, doesn't make it correct. It also doesn't necessarily make me wrong.

Did the Rephaites possess healing powers which later influenced the language? Is there any connection between healing, the Rephaites and the suggested "healing" and balancing purpose of Gilgal Rephaim? We will probably never know.

A megalithic circular structure no one can identify, yet associated with a nation of mysterious Biblical giants, who are in some way connected with spirits and ghosts of the underworld, with weird semantics and stretched etymology. No wonder it threw me into a loop.

The combination of vague notions with solid findings, of mythical and mystic stories with correlations of language, as coincidental as they are probable to be, makes Gilgal Rephaim an endless loop of fascination.

SECRET ISRAEL

PART 2 – THE CENTER

QAQUN

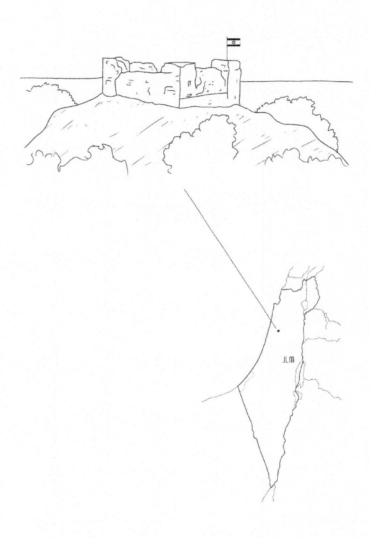

Qaqun

Every week, my dad used to come and pick me up on a Friday afternoon, and take me to spend the weekend with him. Our drives together were always an adventure and I loved talking to him. He was a man of stories, wisdom, and incredible humor. He also had enchanting charisma. Usually, we'd go straight to his home, but sometimes, we'd stop somewhere and have some fun, just the two of us. One day, when I was about fourteen, my dad drove past the turn to the town he lived in.

"Where are we going?" I asked him.

"To breathe some fresh air," Dad said with a smile.

It was less than five minutes of driving until we turned off the road and parked at the bottom of a hill. At the top, I saw the ruins of a fortress. I was always fond of ancient ruins, and could barely resist the temptation of climbing them.

"Cool!" I said. "We're going up there?"

"Yup," my dad said, and grabbed a metal ammo can from the jeep, where he stored his "Outdoor Coffee Kit." Basically a compact gas stove, a small metal kettle and a few tiny glasses tucked in a dirty sock, which according to dad protected them from breaking, as well as added to the flavor. We used to joke around about how he called it his "coffee kit," but all he had in it was Bedouin tea. We started a short climb up the hill and arrived at the fortress.

"Can I climb?" I asked, hoping for a 'yes.'

"Sure, I'll even climb with you," Dad said, and together we climbed to the head of the fortress, handing the ammo can to one another at the tougher climb spots.

Qaqun, 2021. [1]

At the top, a cool breeze welcomed us, and a gorgeous 360-degree view.

"What do you see?" my dad asked.

"The sea", I said, "so that must be the west."

"Correct," Dad said, and pointed to the mountains at the east, across from the sea.

"And these?" he asked.

---

[1] Source: Pikiwiki photo stock. Credit: Udi Steinwall, 2021.

"Mountains", I said embarrassed. Looking back, I may have become a tour guide so that I can always know the answer to the question "What is this?" when asked about anything in Israel.

"These are the mountains of Samaria," dad explained. I was old enough to know that Samaria is part of the mountain ridge of "Judea and Samaria," also known as the "West Bank." I knew it all too well, because dad had lived there when I was younger and we used to hang out with the Palestinians from the nearby village. That was before the second intifada, the Palestinian uprising, broke out in the year 2000 and it became too dangerous to live there. My dad and his family then moved to a town "inside the green line," meaning into what was considered Israeli territory since 1949, and not "an area of dispute." The town he moved to was "on the green line," which meant we were surrounded with a high wall made of cement, and a patrol jeep drove around the gated town on a regular basis to check for infiltrations by terrorists.

"I never realized it was so close," I said.

"Yes, very close. In fact, look over there," my dad said, and pointed southwest, toward the urban area. The day was clear, and I saw what seemed like a carpet of buildings as far as the horizon. "Far over there, that is Tel Aviv, and Petah-Tiqwa, and closer to us is Netanya."

I looked at the mountains of Samaria and then at the Metropolitan of Tel Aviv, where over 4 million people were living. Everything seemed so small.

"Dad", I asked, "what if there's a war?"

This wasn't a baseless question. The year was 2002 and terror attacks of the second intifada were at an alltime high. Suicide bombers blew up in buses, coffee shops, restaurants and malls, trying to kill as many citizens as they could. Over five hundred people were murdered that year. It was a brutal reality to grow up in.

"It is very small, isn't it?" My dad read my mind. "This is one of our biggest challenges these days," he started explaining.

I loved listening to my dad "explain" things. He always had something insightful to say. My sister, my brother and my dad's wife always complained that he was 'lecturing." For me these lectures were a source of endless learning, and I could listen to him talk forever.

"The West Bank is an area under dispute," my dad said. "Some areas in it are controlled by the PNA (Palestinian National Authority), but all of it is under the control and supervision of the IDF and the Israeli government. It is one of the most important assets we have, strategically."

"But dad, who's right in this? Us, or the Arabs?" I asked, and my dad smiled. Since I was about eight-years-old, I used to read the paper every morning with my cereal. My dad knew this and we often used to discuss the news. As much as I liked reading the paper, my dad was my favorite political commentator.

"The Million Dollar Question," my dad said. "For the sake of the argument, let's say that we are right and they are wrong. Do you think they are going anywhere?" He pointed towards the "blanket" of buildings and mosques covering the slopes of the Samaria mountains.

These are people's homes, I thought. Thousands and thousands of them. I don't know them, but I don't want anything bad to happen to them.

"Probably not," I said.

"And for the sake of the same argument, let's say that they are right and we are wrong, do you think all of this is going anywhere?"

He then pointed towards the giant Tel Aviv Metropolitan. I looked directly towards Tel Aviv, where my mom's home was.

"Not a chance," I said while feeling an "inner-fist" of justice tightening up inside of me. I ain't going anywhere. This is my home.

"Well then, it doesn't really matter who's right, does it? No one is going anywhere. Eventually we are going to have to learn how to live here together, assuming most of us don't want the bloodshed, and none of us want to leave," he said. "But until that happens, we have to be able to protect ourselves. Between those mountains of Samaria and the Mediterranean Sea, there are ten miles of flatland. That's it. These are the 'narrow waists' of the State of Israel. Assuming there's a war, it will be very hard to protect ourselves if our enemies are sitting on top of that mountain and we don't have control over it."

In my imagination, I started seeing scenarios of artillery and bombs shooting on the valley separating between the mountains of Samaria and the Mediterranean Sea, the valley where more than half of the population of Israel lives. I didn't like that scenario.

"They don't write about this in the newspaper," I said, trying to process what I just saw and the new knowledge I had gained.

"Nothing is more powerful than seeing with your own eyes," my dad read my thoughts. "The conflict will be solved one day; I truly want to believe that. But until then, our first priority is to survive."

We both stood there, gazing into the beautiful sun that started to set into the sea. It felt like the scene from the Lion King, where Mufasa told Simba that "One day it will all be yours," except reality is harsher than a Disney movie. My "Mufasa moment" with my dad was more like "if we're not careful, we might not survive, we must protect the little we have".

Then we had some Bedouin tea as sweet is life itself, climbed off the fortress, and drove home for Shabbat dinner.

***

About eight years later, as part of my tour guide training program, we visited Qaqun, and I learned that there is a whole lot more to this fortress than just a good vantage point. Though they probably weren't the first on this mountain, the crusaders were the first to leave a structure that survived the tests of time.

Qaqun, 2021 [2]

The foundations of the fortress on the hill were built by the crusaders, who understood the strategic importance of it. In the "bellybutton" of the valley, a lofty hill, even a modest one that's fifty-two meters (one hundred and seventy feet) high, is crucial in

---

[2] Source: Pikiwiki photo stock. Credit: Israel Preker, 2021.

gaining control over the surrounding area. If you can see your enemies coming, you earn a basic advantage over them. The fortress they built was called "Caco", and the name survived, more or less, until today. "Caco" belonged to the Lordship of Caesarea under the Crusaders' Kingdom of Jerusalem. The fortress was ruled by a viscount, and was given as a residency for the Knights Templars to dwell in and protect the Christian pilgrims on their way to Jerusalem.

Despite the crusaders' control over the land, and despite the relative security that ruled the cities, which were surrounded by walls, the roads themselves were far from safe.

Oftentimes, pilgrims to Jerusalem would be attacked, robbed and even murdered by greedy bandits. In order to protect the Christian pilgrimage from Europe to the Holy Land and within the Holy Land to Jerusalem, a group of knights in Jerusalem decided to establish an order to tend to their safety. "The Poor Fellow Soldiers of Christ and the Temple of Solomon," or simply the "Templars," was an order of knights dedicated to the protection and safety of pilgrims heading to the Holy Land. The order was funded by the Kings of Jerusalem and by a vast network of fundraising all over Europe. Soon enough, the order grew, as its necessity was proven crucial not only to protect pilgrims, but also to be sent as shock troops during the continuous battles between the Crusaders and the Ayyubids, a Muslim dynasty led by Saladin.

The tension between the Crusaders Kingdom and the Ayyubid dynasty grew and was finally determined in the Battle of the Horns of Hattin of 1187. The crusaders were brutally beaten by Saladin, the first Kingdom of Jerusalem fell, and the Ayyubid dynasty established its rule in Jerusalem. Nonetheless, the second Kingdom of Jerusalem was soon reestablished with the crusade of King Richard the Lionheart, in 1192. Jerusalem itself was never Christian again, but the second Kingdom of Jerusalem was established in an agreement signed by Saladin and King Richard, and its capital was set in Acre. Christian pilgrims were once again allowed to enter Jerusalem, under Muslim rule.

The Templar order went back to defending the pilgrims on their way to Jerusalem until the appearance of a new power in the region, Sultan Baibars the Mamluk.

Baibars was a leading military commander of the Mamluks sultanate in Egypt. The Mamluks began as non-Muslim soldier-slaves, who were bought, trained and assigned to military positions, first under the Abbasid dynasty, and then around the Muslim world, including the Ayyubid Dynasty in Egypt and the land of Israel. Their purchase made them loyal to the master who bought them as children. Their non-Muslim religion allowed the Muslim rulers to avoid the religious prohibition for one Muslim to fight another Muslim. In Egypt during the Middle Ages, the Mamluks' power grew until eventually they destroyed the Ayyubid dynasty under which they served, and established a Mamluk Sultanate. Baibars, a fearless and decorated Mamluk warrior who was purchased at the early age of 14, became the Mamluk Sultan of Egypt and Damascus. He saw himself as the "torch bearer" following in the footsteps of Saladin the Great, and after defeating the Mongolian infiltration of the Holy Land, he decided to get rid of the crusaders' presence in it once and for all. Unfortunately for the crusaders, he was successful in his mission.

Baibars's attitude was merciless and his strategy was proved useful. In order to prevent the crusaders from ever coming back, he destroyed the glorious chain of barricaded coastline port cities that served as the connecting links between the Kingdom of Jerusalem and its base in Europe. The city of Caesarea, to which Qaqun belonged, was destroyed in 1265.

Qaqun, due to its inland location, wasn't destroyed. On the contrary. Baibars transferred the administrative center of the region from the ruins of Caesarea to Qaqun. He fortified the existing fortress, converted the church that was in it into a mosque, and established a large trade center and a vast postal service, including a popular "line" of homing pigeons.

The strategy of destroying coastal port-cities proved itself to be very efficient. The ports of the Holy Land remained abandoned or small in capacity and functioning, up until the establishment of the British Mandate in the land of Israel in 1918. This prevented any further attempt of Christian or Western infiltration until Napoleon's campaign to the Holy Land in 1799.

By the time Napoleon[3] arrived in the Holy Land, it was already an integral part of the Ottoman Empire, who lost one battle after the other in the fight against him. The same happened in the battle over Qaqun. After his victory in Jaffa (current Tel-Aviv), Napoleon and his army continued to bypass the swamps along the coast line, and made their way through Qaqun, the next  fortress on their way north. On March 15th 1799, Napoleon and his army fought and defeated the Ottoman forces, and continued marching north. In Acre, Napoleon was defeated with the kind help of the British Navy, and the control over the Land of Israel and Qaqun as part of it, was given back to the Ottomans.[4]

---

[3] Photo Source: Public Domain. Napoleon Bonaparte, portrait by Henri Félix Emmanuel Philippoteaux, 1792.
[4] Regev, Y. (2001). *The New Israel Guide*. Volume 6. Yediot Ahronot. Israeli Ministry of Defense. Keter. Jerusalem. Pp. 119-121.

During the time of the Ottoman Empire, 1517 to 1917, and during the short period of rule of Ibrahim Pasha, 1831 to 1840, an Arab village formed around the fortress and on the lands around it. During the 1930s, under the law of the British Mandate in the land, a section was purchased by Joshua Hankin, and was given for the establishment of Kibbutz HaMa'apil. The proximity between the Arab village of Qaqun and the Jewish Kibbutz proved to be fatal in Israel's Independence War in 1948.

During the war, seven Arab armies attacked Israel: Egypt, Syria, Lebanon, Jordan, Saudi Arabia, Iraq, and local Palestinian forces. Qaqun became the post of the Iraqi military to attack Israel. Their post on the hill made them dominant over the entire Hefer valley around it. Despite their strategic advantage, the Alexandroni brigade of the Palmach, the "strike forces" of the Haganah Jewish underground, later to become the IDF, managed to take over the Iraqi post permanently, and gain dominance over the area.

This battle proved to be a turning point in the war over the area. The Iraqi forces acknowledged Israel's dominance over the valley and didn't attack again. As a result, when the war ended and the borders of the new country of Israel were determined, the valley was declared as Israeli territory "inside the green line," according to the borders set in the truce of 1949.

The Arab village of Qaqun vanished after the war. The Arab residents of the village escaped the war and fled to the mountain of Samaria. At the end of the war, Samaria remained in the hands of the Kingdom of Jordan. Anyone who escaped during the war, be it Jews who escaped Arab countries into Israel or Arabs who fled from what became Israeli territory to the neighboring countries such as Jordan or Lebanon, weren't allowed to return home.

Samaria remained under Jordanian control until the Six-Day War in 1967, when Israel managed to establish dominance over the hills of Judea and Samaria, and the Kingdom of Jordan withdrew east of the Jordan river. The valley around Qaqun was settled with a chain of towns and villages who farmed almost the entire valley. In the peace accord signed between the State of Israel and the Kingdom of Jordan, the King of Jordan gave up the area and left it for Israel. The mountain ridge of Judea and Samaria, also known as "The West Bank" (of the Jordan River), were declared and still are, an area under dispute.

Unfortunately, the conflict between Israel and the Palestinian authority continues, in which the Palestinian authority demands the return of the Palestinians to the lands they once lived in, and the State of Israel demands recognition in its right to exist in peace. Needless to say, neither side has ever agreed to give up its demands.

Ten years after that visit to Qaqun with my dad, I started guiding my first groups and was often asked about the conflict and Israel's legitimacy in it. Every time that happened, I wished I could take my visitors to Qaqun to see the topography of the land with their own eyes. Defending the State of Israel is one of the hardest challenges in the world, and the physical configuration of the land makes it easier to understand.

The Israeli-Palestinian or Jewish-Arab conflict, depending on who you ask, is one of the most "covered" and "populized" conflicts in the world, and more times than not, Israel is portrayed as the "oppressor" or the "prosecutor." Most people want the truth they think they know to be pure and simple. Unfortunately, "the truth is never pure, and rarely simple"[5]. Instead, it is a messy cluster of

---

[5] Oscar Wilde.

contradictory facts and narratives that are far too close to one another with little harmony or hope for a better future.

Qaqun, 2021 [6]

When dad died, we buried him in the cemetery closest to Qaqun. Almost every time when I go visit my dad's tomb, I drive to Qaqun right after and climb the hill, like I did with my father when I was younger. So many great leaders conquered this place. They understood the value of the land and the importance of it. When I stand up there at the one-thousand-year-old crusader's fortress, I wonder about our place in the chain of generations and in the chain of conflicts this country has known and will probably continue to know, for many, many years to come.

By seeing with our own eyes, we may not be able to bring a conflict to an end, but we can start containing the complexity of it, and that's something. I think my dad knew that by bringing me there, simple questions about good and evil would become a comprehensive understanding of a multidimensional problem. Only by fully understanding the problem can we start being a part of the solution.

---

[6] Source: Pikiwiki photo stock. Credit: Israel Preker, 2021.

CISTERN OF ARCHES

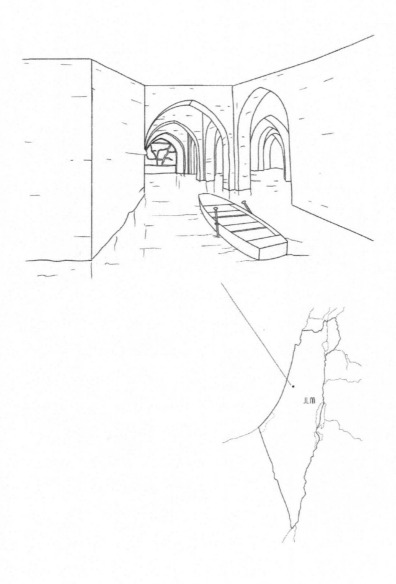

Cistern of Arches

"Who's Hades?" my sister's colleague asked, looking at my sister's ringing phone with an expression of surprise.

"My sister", my sister replied, referring to me. It was I who called her phone, and in there I am written under the name "Hades." She in return is saved in my phone under the name "Zeus".

The whole thing started with a silly joke by our dad. When my sister was younger, she used to spend hours and hours in her room upstairs. My brother's obsession with the Disney movie "Hercules" (and by obsession, I mean that even today, my family could probably recite the entire movie backwards, just from overhearing it so many times) soon inspired my dad to call my sister's room upstairs "Olympus." She was often kindly asked to climb down from her lofty throne up there, and join us, the simpletons, down in the common room.

When we started to call her Zeus, she gave me the nickname "Hades." The nickname reflected both my bedroom's location downstairs, opposite of hers, and I'm pretty sure it had something to do with what she thought of my personality. Either way, the names were forever commemorated in our phones, for generations to come.

"Hey Zeus," I said when she picked up. "Want to come with me to a prep tour?"

Before I go guiding in places I haven't been to for a while, I always make sure to go on a prep tour. It helps me collect my thoughts about the guiding, as well as to avoid surprises. My friends and family usually get the benefit of joining me for some quality time, and get a free tour on the way. My sister, who also has a secret affection for traveling through history, is a fan of these opportunities.

"Cool! Yes, of course. Where to?" She asked.

"Ramla!" I said, anticipating this wasn't going to go over well.

"No, seriously! Where to?" she repeated.

"Ramla!" I insisted.

"For real? Like the prison?" she asked with clear contempt in her tone.

"Like the prison, except not the prison, but the city it was named after, right next to it" I answered.

This wasn't going to go down without a fight, and my sister, I knew, is the one person who would get a real kick out of where I wanted to go.

"Are you sure you don't have to do a prep tour in a place that isn't famous for not being famous?" she asked.

"Come on, sis," I begged. "I promise it will be worth your time. Plus," I added, as part of my scheme to convince her, "I am scared to go there alone. You know how much I hate going underground."

"Give me one good reason to go."

"What if I told you that if you come with me, I can prove to you that the source for all the Gothic culture you like so much, is in Ramla?" I asked, knowing I'd hit the spot.

"In Ramla?" she asked.

"Not just in Ramla, but underneath Ramla!" I declared with confidence.

"Now that I think about it, it isn't that hard to believe that hell would be underneath Ramla. Fine. I'll come. But this better be good!" She warned me.

"I promise you, Zeus, not only are you going to follow Hades to hell, I can guarantee a boat sail through the river of dead souls!" I performed my role a bit too enthusiastically.

"Yeah, I'll come but don't push it," she said, and I could hear her laughing before she hung up the phone.

The next Saturday, my sister and I met for our tour.

"So far, it looks glorious," she said cynically, looking around.

Ramla is one of those places that would play you for a fool. As a city in Israel, it doesn't have the best reputation, and that's an understatement.

For a big part of my military service, I was positioned and working in a military prison for IDF soldiers. Part of my job was to visit the inmates' families in their homes, estimate their socioeconomic condition and recommend aid if necessary. Unfortunately, I can testify that a good number of my home visits were done in Ramla. The stigma I had about the place wasn't just based on what I'd heard, but of what I'd seen with my own eyes. For a while, Ramla seemed to me like a poor, neglected, dangerous place with a bad reputation for having crime, gangs, and drugs.

That all changed when I finished my military service, and had the good fortune to follow my beloved teacher and mentor, Dr. Shimon Gat, who always seemed to me like an old and wise sea lion. Shimon has been researching Ramla for decades and knows it like the back of his hand. It took one tour with him to change the image of Ramla in my head from a hell hole to a hidden gem. Shimon did to me what I believe should be the mission of every tour guide out there - reveal the unseen beauty. I decided to take upon myself the mission of paying it forward, and my sister, luckily for her, was about to be my first guinea pig.

"So why are we here? What's the prep tour for?" she asked.

"Well, I have a couple coming over, and one of them is an architect. They asked me to take them to see cool architectural sights in Israel," I said.

"And you thought Ramla was the way to go?" my sister asked, and sounded surprised.

"You'd be surprised, Zeus," I said. "But Ramla has more to it than meets the eye."

"I know. They can't sell drugs in sheer daylight. It's illegal", she said.

"Hilarious" I replied.

"But seriously now, isn't impressive architecture usually connected with King Herod the Great? Or the Crusaders? What on earth are we doing in Ramla? No joke now, I'm curious," my sister said.

"Well, as far as the 'western narrative', you're right. But the beauty about Israel is that it is the meeting point between cultures. This is where east meets west, where the desert in the south meets the green lands of the north and where Christianity meets Islam,"

I said. "Ramla is the product of the first establishment of a Muslim Caliphate in the Holy Land."

"Yeah, when exactly did the Muslims join the Holy-Land party?" My sister asked.

"Well, Islam started officially in the year 622, and was established by Muhamad in the cities of Mecca and Medina. After he died, in 632, his successors after him were appointed as caliph, which simply means replacer, or heir in Arabic. The first four caliphs were elected with some general agreement, and the second one, Omar, went on a very successful campaign west, against the Byzantines. He conquered Iraq, Syria, Egypt, and Israel. Before Omar, the Byzantine empire, which is basically the Roman empire converted to Christianity, ruled the land after 325 AD. When Omar arrived to the Holy Land in 638 AD, he established it as a Muslim land and built a mosque on top of the Temple Mount."

"Is that the Dome of the Rock?" my sister asked.

"Almost, but not quite," I answered. "You see, before Omar got here, the Temple Mount was basically a garbage dump. When Omar arrived, he recognized the Temple Mount with a site in the Quran that tells about Muhammad's ascension to heaven. The Quran doesn't mention Jerusalem by name, it just calls it 'The mosque that is far away'. Nonetheless, Omar decided that the Temple Mount is the right identification for this event, and built his mosque, but the mosque he built was made out of wood and didn't survive. The Dome of the Rock however, was built by the Muslim dynasty that was established a few years after Omar died. The Umayyad Muslim Dynasty."

"So they were the first Muslim caliphate in the Holy Land?"

"Yes. The Umayyad dynasty settled its capital in Damascus, declared the land of Israel as a "Jund," a district of its own, and invested quite a lot in constructing it. The Dome of the Rock is only one of the magnificent structures they built[1], and it's still here! Ramla was another project of the Umayyad dynasty."

"So they're responsible for both the Dome of the Rock and Ramla? I've got to say that so far, I am not very happy with their brand", she chuckled.

"Wow! You're in a mood today!" I said, amused.

"Aren't I always?" she laughed. "But seriously, you brought me to Ramla for a tour, so I'm waiting to see when I am getting my money's worth," she teased.

"Well, when the Umayyad dynasty was established, they didn't want to use the same cities that the Byzantines used for their center. They wanted to 'start fresh,' and also demonstrate their strength in the region as a Muslim superpower. They decided that instead of using an existing city, they would build the capital and administrative center for the region from scratch. They established Ramla, and according to travelers' literature from that time, it was one of the richest and most glorious cities in the area. It had markets, hostels and bathhouses. The houses were coated with carved marble and Ramla was famous for its olive oil, figs and fabric industry."

My sister looked around at the poor looking buildings of the old city. "I'm sorry," she said, "but these don't look like the remains of a glorious city".

"You are right, sis. Ramla has had bad luck," I explained. "The Umayyad dynasty thought they chose a prime location. Right on the crossroads on the way from Jaffa to Jerusalem (the gateway from the west) and right on the way leading from Egypt in the

---

[1] 691 AD

south to Syria in the north. Supposedly, what could have been better? Alas, while the city was flawlessly structured, what they couldn't have known is that they built their city on a center of massive tectonic activity. Ramla was destroyed by earthquakes time and time again. The earthquake of 1033 destroyed a third of the city, and the one that followed in 1068 destroyed the rest. Fifteen thousand people were killed in that earthquake, and whoever survived fled the city."[2]

"So who rebuilt it?" Zeus asked me.

"The Seljuk dynasty" I answered.

"Oh, were they here after the Umayyad dynasty?" She tried putting the pieces together.

"No, that was the Abbasid dynasty." I remained true to the history.

"Well now you're just making stuff up to mess with me," she said and I laughed.

"I swear I ain't making anything up," I laughed. "The Early Muslim period is like that, especially in the land of Israel. In history it is marked between the years 638 and 1099 as 'The Early Muslim Period,' which is basically between the Byzantine Empire and the arrival of the crusaders in 1099. Nonetheless, this era was filled with wars between different Arab tribes, Muslim dynasties, and between Sunni and Shiite Islam. I think it is safe to say that in four hundred years of Muslim dominance in the region, every dynasty lasted about one hundred years or much less."

---

[2] Gat, S. (n.d.). *The Story of Ramla, the City that Wandered.* Ramla Municipality's Official Website.

"Ok, so the city was rebuilt by...?" She tried weaving the details back together.

"The Seljuks" I answered. "But it was destroyed again in the earthquake of 1546".

"So basically, great idea - lousy execution," my sister summed it up poetically.

"Bingo," I laughed. "However, while the entire city was destroyed and rebuilt again and again, one structure did survive, and that's where I wanted to take you today."

We kept going until we arrived at a blue gate and walked into a courtyard. The yard had rows of half-cylinders carved from stone on the ground, and on top of them were little square holes drilled in evenly apart from one another.

"This is it?" my sister asked, disappointed.

"You're a spoiled Olympus brat, Zeus," I teased her. "To explore Hades's kingdom, you must go down yonder, to the damp depths of darkness," I started acting again and led her to the entrance of what seemed like a tiny white chamber, that only contained a stairwell going down. "After you, Zeusi," I bowed and gave my sister the honor of going down first.

"What's down there?" She looked at me with suspicion before walking down the stairs. My sister and I have a history of pranking one another, and over the years, it may have tainted the trust between us.

"A water cistern," I said innocently.

"So, we're going to visit Ramla's sewer?"

"Yes," I said amused, willing to say anything for her to go down there already. "It's Ramla's sewer. We have a meeting with the Ramla branch of the Ninja Turtles. Now would you please just go downstairs?"

"Ok, but if they're really there, I call dibs on Donatello," she said laughing, bringing back our old childhood feud.

"Not a chance!" I called behind her as she started going down the stairs. "He's mine!"

"Wow!" she gasped as she got to the bottom of the stairs and finally saw 'The underworld of Ramla' with her own eyes.

Cistern of Arches, 2015. [3]

A vast hall, about half a dunam (0.12 acres) in size revealed itself under the ground, all covered in water. We were standing on a small wooden dock built close to the stairs and everything around us was surrounded by water. The entire place was held by giant stone vaults that were nine meters (thirty feet) high. A small

---

[3] Source: Pikiwiki photo stock. Credit: Dr, Avishai Teicher, 2015.

wooden row boat was floating near the dock, and my sister looked confused.

"This is incredible! Did I die and go to hell?" she said.

"Not yet, but one day - likely," I teased. "Looking for Cerberus?" I referenced Hades's threeheaded guarding dog from the Greek mythology.

"No kidding!" she replied, still gazing around, trying to take it all in. "A gothic structure underneath Ramla? This is just awesome!"

"I knew you'd appreciate it," I said.

"Ok, I want you to tell me all about it, but first - to the boat!" she shouted and hopped into the rowboat while her voice kept echoing between the vaults. I was thrilled to see her so excited and got in the boat with her.

"On, Charon!" she ordered, as if I was the ferryman of the river to the underworld.

"How can I be both Charon and Hades?" I wasn't going to let her get away with this.

"I'm Zeus, you are what I say you are!" she said.

"Ok Zeusi, now take an oar and start rowing," I teased back.

"Ok, I'll row but you tell the story. What is this place?" she asked, while rowing the boat and getting us away from the dock and into the specious cistern.

I knew this would get her all excited. Ever since my sister and I were young, we had a slight affection for fantasy and the dark worlds. As we grew up, I took more of an interest in the historical side while my sister remained a huge fan of fantasy, goth culture and mystery in general. This was just the place for her.

I took a deep breath and began telling her the story. My voice carried and echoed all over the cistern and the whole experience felt pretty mystical.

"Well", I began, "in the year 750 AD, the Abbasid dynasty kindled a revolution and overthrew the Umayyad dynasty from its throne. The center of the Muslim world then moved from Damascus in Syria, to Bagdad, the capital of Iraq. In the year 789 AD, during the days of Harun al-Rashid, the fifth caliph of the Abbasid caliphate, an order was given to build this water cistern to provide drinking water to the people of Ramla and the industries surrounding it. The water comes from the aquifer beneath us, and the holes you see above our heads," I pointed to the little holes in the ceiling that we saw on top of the stone cylinders before we went down to the cistern "were used for canisters, to collect the water and bring them above ground[4]".

"Nope" my sister suddenly said.

"Excuse me?" I wasn't sure what was the source of her resistance, given that she was never here before, and didn't know who the Abbasids were five minutes ago.

"No", she repeated and explained, "this place couldn't have been built by the Muslims in the eighth century. These pointed top arches" she pointed with her finger to the top of the many arches that supported the cistern, "are Gothic architecture. They only started using them around the thirteenth century, and this is

---

[4] Gat, S. (n.d.). *Many Cisterns and One Aqueduct - The Water Supply to Ancient Ramla.*
Gat, S. (n.d.).

European architecture. So I don't think you've got your story right."

My sister, of course, was absolutely right. Pointed arches only became popular around Europe in the thirteenth century and were the base for the Gothic architecture of many world-famous buildings, like the church of Notre Dame. It was this architecture that inspired Gothic art and centuries later, inspired Gothic literature and Gothic culture.

"Now how exactly do you know that?" I was impressed. This wasn't common knowledge.

"Too much Edgar Allen Poe, I suppose," my sister smiled. She is the worst bookworm in our family. After working in the public library since she was fourteen, none of us were able to compete with her "book mileage." She was always leaning more towards literature about the dark and mysterious. On second thought, I guess it is no surprise she knew how to recognize and date Gothic arches.

"You are absolutely right sis," I said, "and still, I'm going to prove you wrong. When this place was discovered, an inscription in Arabic was revealed on the walls. It is dated to the Abbasid dynasty, and describes the order given to build this cistern. However, allow me to complete a small piece of the historical puzzle," I continued. "Arches in general were very popular in Roman architecture. They left us impressive architecture, with the arch as a central element in it. The Romans mainly used the semicircular arch, which is the classic arch most of us know. The arch itself is a pretty revolutionary element in architecture. The compression-form structure of it allows it to carry heavy weights for a long time, by shifting it to the base of the arch. The pointed arch however, was an amazing innovation, because the arch action produces less horizontal thrust at the bases of it. This allowed architects to 'upgrade' their structures to be taller and with more spacious openings, which soon became what we all know as 'Gothic Architecture'. That's why the 'Pointed Arch' is also more commonly known as the 'Gothic Arch.'"

"See? I told you I was right!" My sister bragged.

"Almost sis, almost," I chuckled. "You see, not all the architects in history agreed that this arch should be called the 'Gothic Arch,'" I said as we floated peacefully between the pointed vaults. "Christopher Wren for instance, was an English polymath, and one of England's most famous architects. He claimed that the Gothic Arch should be called the 'Saracen Arch'[5], after the Muslims who developed it and used it quite a bit during the Muslim Golden Age. This Golden Age started, surprise surprise, during the days of Harun al-Rashid, and ended with the Mongolian invasion which brought to the destruction of the Abbasid dynasty in 1258."

"So what you're saying is that Gothic architecture is basically a Muslim invention? That's wild," she seemed fascinated. "So what did he say it should be called? The 'what' arch?"

"'Saracen,'" I repeated. "Saracen was the name the crusaders used to describe their various Muslim enemies in the Holy Land. The first Europeans to use the pointed arch were actually crusaders in the Holy Land. Back then the style was called 'Romanesque.' They brought this method and style of building back to Europe with them. Later on the name changed into 'Gothic'. But nonetheless, the Crusaders developed their unique building style from the 'Saracen Arch' that they first saw here."

---

[5] Bolton, A. T., ed. (1925). *"St Paul's Cathedral"*. The Wren Society. Oxford University Press. Pp: 15–20.

"In the Holy Land!" my sister emphasized.

"No, no," I insisted. "**Here**."

"You mean right here?" she asked, surprised.

Cistern of Arches, 2015. [6].

"Well", I said, "that, I obviously can't know for sure. What I do know though, is that the crusaders did live here in Ramla. We have broad documentation of it. I also know that this is the only Abbasid structure in Israel. And last, but most importantly, this structure is probably the most ancient example of pointed arches known in Islamic architecture worldwide[7]. So, with some caution, I think we can assume..."

"That Gothic architecture started in a cistern underneath Ramla!" My sister completed my sentence with enthusiasm.

---

[6] Source: Pikiwiki photo stock. Credit: Dr, Avishai Teicher, 2015.
[7] Avni, G. (2011). *Continuity and change in the cities of Palestine during the Early Islamic period.*

"Correcto!" I shared her joy. "Ramla, the Umayyad and Abbasid city that was destroyed again and again, is the birthplace of the architectural element that created one of the most famous, stable and long-lasting building methods in Europe. Underneath Ramla is the source for every Gothic building and the root of every Gothic story you read. So how's that for a visit to Ramla?" I asked filled with pride.

"Not too bad!" my sister said with her scheming smile. 'Uh oh' I thought as my instincts warned me she was up to something, but I couldn't tell what. "For a visit to hell!" she shouted laughing as she pushed me off the boat.

"You little devil!" I shouted as I rose from the water and returned the favor, by flipping the boat with her in it.

Needless to say, neither of us left the cistern dry.

SECRET ISRAEL

PART 3 – JERUSALEM

SECRET ISRAEL

ABSALOM'S TOMB

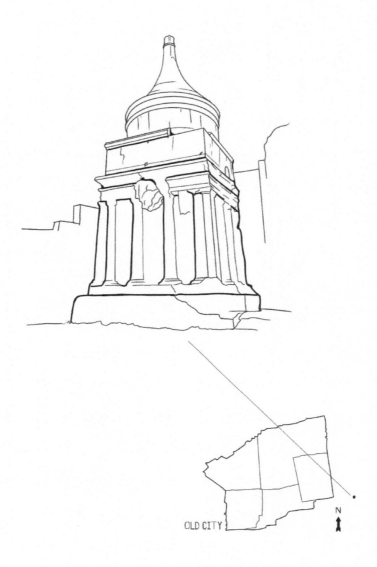

OLD CITY

N

Absalom's Tomb

Between the Mount of Olives and the Temple Mount, down from Gethsemane and along the road from the neighborhood of Silwan, below the Golden Gate and under the shadow of the City of David, and downhill from the Jewish graves covering the mountain, are the Tombs of Kidron Valley. Those who walk among them, are walking on a ground from 2,000 ago, and probably more.

The area surrounding the tomb is one of the most layered, ancient and clamored-for pieces of the Holy Land. Around it are Biblical remains buried under generations of construction and population in Jerusalem, yet the ancient monuments have stood lofty and visible since the day they were carved, throughout two thousand years of history.

The location of the Necropolis of Kidron Valley, right beneath the city of David and the current ancient city of Jerusalem, is not coincidental. The ancient pharaohs of Egypt built the known pyramids in the west side of the Nile River, where the sun sets, in the dry and barren desert, which they referred to as "The Realm of the Dead."

It's hard to ignore the similarity to that in the location of Jerusalem itself. Divine intervention aside, Jerusalem is located on the seam line between the populated and fertile land and the desert. Mount Moriah and the temple are gazing above Kidron Valley, which in many ways *is* "The Realm of the Dead" of the Holy Land. Kidron valley starts in the old city of Jerusalem, and drains into the Dead Sea, in the barren Judean Desert. The valley connects Jerusalem with the oh-so-near desert, symbolizing danger, vapidity and death. In the south-east corner of Jerusalem, Kidron valley meets the "Valley of Ben Hinnom":

> *"... 'They have set up their detestable idols in the house that bears my Name and have defiled it... They have built the high places of Topheth in the Valley of Ben Hinnom to burn their sons and daughters in the fire... "*

> **- *Jeremiah 7:30-31 NIV***

Gai Ben Hinnom, 1900. [1]

The Valley of Ben Hinnom, or in Hebrew, "Gai Ben-Hinnom," is known to be the place where pagans used to sacrifice children to the Moloch. The name "Gai Ben-Hinnom" is very close to one of the Hebrew words for Hell - "Gehenom". The Mishnah (Jewish commentary over the Torah, 200 AD) mentions that one of the three gateways to hell is in Jerusalem[2] (the other two are in the sea

---

[1] Source: Public Domain
[2] Babylonian Talmud, Tractate Eruvin, 19a

and the desert), and following the prophecies of Jeremiah, there are those who believe, even today, that The Valley of Ben-Hinnom may be the gateway to hell:

> *This is what the Lord says... go out to the Valley of Ben Hinnom... There, proclaim the words I tell you, and say, 'Hear the word of the Lord, you kings of Judah and people of Jerusalem. This is what the Lord Almighty, the God of Israel, says: Listen! I am going to bring a disaster on this place... For they have forsaken me... and they have filled this place with the blood of the innocent. They have built the high places of Baal to burn their children... So beware, the days are coming, declares the Lord, when people will no longer call this place Topheth or the Valley of Ben Hinnom, but the Valley of Slaughter..."*

> **-   *Jeremiah 19:1-6 NIV***

Setting aside the connection to the Valley of Ben-Hinnom and the hellish associations it brings with it, Kidron Valley is mentioned ten times in the Old Testament and once in the New Testament, always in connection with death, sorrow, and doom. It was often the place where the righteous kings of Judah burned the idols they found in the kingdom (2 Kings 23, 2 Chronicles 15, 29 and 30). In the New Testament it is mentioned as the place where Jesus was arrested:

> *"When he had finished praying, Jesus left with his disciples and crossed the Kidron Valley. On the other side there was a garden, and he and his disciples went into it..."*

> **-   *John 18:1 NIV***

Indeed, it is well established that right outside the Golden Gate to the Temple, lies a valley of death and doom. The first mention of Kidron Valley however, is the story of Absalom, the rebellious son of King David.

There are several monumental burial structures in Kidron Valley. The tomb of Pharaoh's Daughter, the tomb of Zechariah, or the tomb of Benei Hezir of the Temple's priestly division. None however, are as famous or bear as many stories, in my opinion, as the tomb of Absalom.

It's true that the scriptures don't paint Absalom in the best light, but I must admit I always had a warm place in my heart for him. Maybe it's because that among my many sins, I've always had a weakness for a rebellious, charismatic and somewhat heroic character with a gorgeous head of hair -

> *"Whenever he cut the hair of his head—he used to cut his hair once a year because it became too heavy for him—he would weigh it, and its weight was two hundred shekels by the royal standard."*
>
> - ***2 Samuel 14:26 NIV***

Maybe it's because I liked the fact that he looked after his sister, Tamar, and killed their brother Amnon for raping her.

> *"...Amnon is dead. This has been Absalom's express intention ever since the day Amnon raped his sister Tamar."*
>
> - ***2 Samuel 13:32 NIV***

Absalom's Soldiers Killing Amnon for Raping Tamar, 1728 [3]

My heart went out for him when I read about the awful way he died.

> *"He was riding his mule, and as the mule went under the thick branches of a large oak, Absalom's hair got caught in the tree. He was left hanging in midair, while the mule he was riding kept on going... Joab... took three javelins in his hand and plunged them into Absalom's heart while Absalom was still alive in the oak tree. And ten of Joab's armor-bearers surrounded Absalom, struck him and killed him..."*

> -   ***2 Samuel 18:9-14 NIV***

---

[3] Source: Public domain, Engraving from a French book, 1728.

Absalom's Death, 1762. [4]

Despite my personal fondness for Absalom, everyone likes an underdog. His name became connected with undermining and rebelling against one's father. Either way, he is a Biblical figure that's hard to forget.

Maybe this is why, despite the fact that other sons of David (except Solomon of course) had their names disappear without leaving a physical trace, the name of Absalom survived in Jerusalem for generations, not just through scripture, but through an impressive, rock-carved monolithic monument, that he himself never built.

"The Tomb of Absalom" is a name given to an unusual monumental tombstone, standing out in the barren Kidron Valley, just south from the garden of Gethsemane and the Golden Gate.

---

[4] Source: Public domain, Spanish artwork, 1762

Absalom's Monument, 2009. [5]

---

[5] Source: Pikiwiki photo stock. Credit: Yigal Zalmanson, 2009

The monument is sixty-six feet or 19.7 meters tall and hewn from the soft chalk rock of the Mount of Olives. The bottom part of the monument is a monolith, while the upper part is built of ashlars. The bottom part is a square-shaped base with ionic pilasters[6] decorating the walls around it. The base is crowned with a Doric frieze of triglyphs and metopes and an Egyptian cornice.

The ashlar-built part is made of three segments. A square base on top of the Egyptian cornice, a round drum with a rope-shaped decoration around it and a "cone"-shaped "hat", topped with a half-closed lotus flower ornament, with six petals.

The inside of the tomb is mostly hollow, with a staircase leading inside and a burial chamber with arcosolium graves carved from the bottom monolith.

Ionic? Doric? Egyptian? Why the mix of architectural styles? How do we know it wasn't Absalom who's buried there? And if not Absalom, then who?

All excellent questions (with tourists being absent as I write these words, I make due with constructive self dialogue). Architecturally, the tomb has an ancient eclectic style to it. As mentioned in the introduction, the land of Israel is uniquely located as a crossroads between continents, which often made it a meeting point of empires and cultures, from ancient times until nowadays. Many empires that took over the land left cultural marks in architecture that we can still trace today in archeological research. It is not unusual, for instance, to excavate Roman structures with spectacular patterns of Egyptian mosaic floors in them. The combination of architectural styles may indicate a

---

[6] A decorative element originating in ancient Greek architecture - 'half pillars' carved out from the rock that makes the wall. At times used as means of support and at times for decoration. Commonly used in Roman architecture as well.

multicultural persona who ordered this monument, or perhaps an attempt to demonstrate power, wealth and greatness for centuries and apparently millenniums to come.

So who is buried there and how do we know it wasn't Absalom? If it wasn't him, why is the place called "Absalom's Tomb?" When archeologists first came to the Holy Land from Europe during the 19th Century, the land was a godforsaken region in the progressively dissolving Ottoman empire.

Imagine coming to a land that is faltering and undeveloped, with no research institutions, universities or high-scholars. A land where the majority of the "historical" knowledge is based on oral traditions passed from generation to generation, and ancient Muslim, Christian, and Jewish religious scriptures that only a handful of local religious leaders knew how to find or read. Under those conditions, the European archeologists faced the first challenge of their work: assigning the correct identification to the right find.

When archeologists, scholars or any travelers curious about the Holy Land arrived in it in the 19th Century, they would often be assigned a local Arab guide and a translator. Wandering alone in the land back then was far from safe. The local guide would usually brief the scholar about local traditions regarding the different sites. They crossed-referenced the information they got with older written sources they had about the Holy Land, such as Travelers' Journals, Crusaders' documents, Roman documents, and of course, the Bible.

When the first archeologists arrived in the Holy Land in the 19th Century, Titus Tobler, Charles Clermont-Ganneau and others, they found Absalom's Tomb partially "buried" under a giant pile of rocks. The local Arabs used to call this monument "Pharaoh's Hat" or even "Pharaoh's Kettle", probably due to its uncommon cone shaped top, reminiscent of a pyramid. However, since the 10th or 11th Century, the place was known as "Absalom's Tomb"[7] in traveler's journals, based on biblical scripture:

> *"During his lifetime Absalom had taken a pillar and erected it in the King's Valley as a monument to himself, for he thought, "I have no son to carry on the memory of my name." He named the pillar after himself, and it is called Absalom's Monument to this day"*

> -   ***2 Samuel 18:18 NIV***

Travelers and locals alike began associating the fancy, yet oddly shaped structure, with the monument Absalom built for himself. The biblical story is not very consistent with Absalom's life story. Four chapters before Absalom's tragic death, the Bible describes him as a father of three sons and one beautiful daughter, whom he probably named after his cruelly defiled sister:

> *"Three sons and a daughter were born to Absalom. His daughter's name was Tamar, and she became a beautiful woman."*

> -   ***2 Samuel 14:27 NIV***

Why then, did Absalom remain without sons and had to build a monument to preserve his memory? The answer remains a mystery. However, the tradition kept recognizing the mentioned "King's Valley" as "Kidron Valley", and the monumental structure as Absalom's Tomb.

Another odd tradition was tied with Absalom's name and the tomb.

---

[7] Breslavi, Y. (1964). *Jerusalem's Guide from the Cairo Genizah*. The Company for the Research of the Land of Israel and its Antiquities, Israel.

It appears that since at least the 15th Century, the tomb became a local "pilgrimage" site of sorts, a place where fathers took their mischievous, misbehaving sons to teach them the fate of rebellious sons.

Absalom's Monument, before excavation, 1898-1914. [8]

According to records left by Felix Fabri, a Swiss Dominican theologian who traveled the land in the 15th Century, fathers of Jerusalem, Muslims, Christians and Jews alike, would bring their sons to stand in front of the monument. There, they would tell them the story of Absalom, and encourage them to spit and cast stones at the monument of the wicked son[9]. Why cast stones? It is safe to assume that this custom originated in the verse describing how in order to further punish him even after his tragic death, Absalom's body wasn't spared, and he was never given a proper burial:

---

[8] Source: Publick Domain. 1898-1914
[9] Eish Shalom, M. (1965). *Christian Pilgrimages to the Land of Israel.* Am-Oved & Dvir. Tel-Aviv. Pp. 249-250.

"They took Absalom, threw him into a big pit in the forest and piled up a large heap of rocks over him"

- ***2 Samuel 18:17 NIV***

Indeed, when the archeologists arrived at the monument, their first task was to clear out the giant pile of rocks and stones that were cast at it, as well as empty the tomb of the stones that had made their way inside.

A thorough examination of the structure's architecture by experts (specifically Prof. Nachman Avigad) determined beyond any doubts, that despite the well rooted tradition about Absalom, the monument was built in the 1st Century AD, more than 1,000 years after Absalom had died (approximately 1,000 BC).

Funnily enough, it appears that stories can grow stories. The tale of the tomb of Absalom took off and tied itself to Jewish tradition, and even to Napoleon Bonaparte. A few decades after his journey to the Holy Land, a legend began to travel, saying Napoleon had paid a visit to Absalom's tomb and had not spared the rebellious son his fury.

According to the legend, Napoleon aimed his cannon at the top of the tomb and blew up an ornament shaped like a palm of a hand that was carved at the top of the cone, all while yelling "Off with the hand that rebelled against its father!"

Why palm-shaped of all shapes? Well, the Hebrew word for "monument" is spelled יד (Yad), which also means "hand" or "palm." The Tomb of Absalom is called "Yad Avshalom" in Hebrew, and the double meaning of "palm" and "monument" must have generated this very far-fetched legend. How can we be sure that this story never happened? The top of the monument is still whole, with a beautiful lotus flower carved on it. Plus, Napoleon never made it to Jerusalem.[10]

Absalom wasn't the only name tied with this monument. Different travelers to the Holy Land identified it as the tomb of different historical and holy figures. Some claim it was the tomb of St. Simon, others claim it was King Hezekiah or Jehoshaphat (whose tomb was found right next to this monument), and even as the tomb of Jacob, Jesus's brother.

In 2003, an anthropologist named Jo Zias was helping one of his students with her paper about Absalom's tomb, when suddenly he noticed that in one of the old photos she was examining, there may have been an inscription on the tomb[11]. At first, Zias was ignored by his fellow scholars and archeologists, claiming that the research done on the tomb was thorough and of the highest quality. Nonetheless, Zias couldn't let go of the feeling something was there. He located the photographer, a renowned professional photographer of archeology, who had taken the photograph decades earlier.

The photographer went with him to the tomb, but they didn't see anything and didn't find the inscription. Zias was close to giving up on the entire thing, but Ze'ev Radoven the photographer encouraged him to keep his observations on the tomb. Sometimes, he explained, the hour of the day and the specific angle in which the light falls upon the object, can bring out things never seen before.

Almost every day, the retired anthropologist sat in front of the tomb, reading a book and taking a photo every hour. It took two

[10] Morgenstern, A. (2006). *Hastening Redemption: Messianism and Resettlement of the Land of Israel.* Oxford University Press. Pp. 11.

[11] Karpel, D. (2003). *One Day, The Letters Came Out.* Ha'aretz.

years, until one day, pale and almost completely worn out, the inscription popped out. With the help of his colleagues, Zias finally deciphered the inscription:

This is the tomb of Zachariah, the martyr, the holy priest, the father of John.

So is this it? Did the tomb reveal itself to be the tomb of Zechariah, the father of John the Baptist? Unfortunately, no.

The inscription was dated to the 4th Century AD, approximately three hundred years after the death of Zechariah. By whom? Possibly by Byzantine monks who used the monument as a small place of worship, or perhaps as a cell for hermits. They recognized the monument as the tomb of Zachariah, father of John the Baptist and carved the inscription on the tomb, regardless of the fact that Zachariah was never a martyr.

However, a neighboring burial monument in Kidron Valley "just down the road" from Absalom's Tomb, is known as "The Tomb of Zechariah", with an interesting story of its own. Thus, it appears that there were other traditions tying the burial of Zechariah to one of these monuments, and it wasn't necessarily Zechariah the father of John the Baptist. Some assume it was Zechariah son of Jehoiada the priest, who was a martyr:

"Then the Spirit of God came on Zechariah son of Jehoiada the priest. He stood before the people and said, "This is what God says: 'Why do you disobey the Lord's commands? You will not prosper. Because you have forsaken the Lord, he has forsaken you.'" But they plotted against him, and by order of the king they stoned him to death in the courtyard of the Lord's temple.

- ***2 Chronicles 24:20-21 NIV***

Zechariah Ben Jehoyada Killed by King's Orders, 19ᵗʰ/20ᵗʰ Century. [12]

It seems it was neither Absalom or Zachariah in the tomb. So who's buried in this unusual structure? In researching history and archeology, until an inscription carved in stone and dated to the right era naming the person who was buried in this monument is found, we will probably never know, but that doesn't mean we can't make educated guesses. The best, last, and most educated and popular one yet, was made by Prof. Gabi Barkai.

---

[12] Source: Publick Domain. Credit: William Hole, 19ᵗʰ/20ᵗʰ Century

In 2013, Prof. Barkai published his research connecting the monument with King Herod the Great's grandson, King Herod Agripa. The recent historic discovery of King Herod's tomb in Herodion in 2006, helped Barkai find similarities in the patterns of architecture and burial, not to mention that the dating of the monument to the 1st century AD, aligns perfectly with the death of King Herod Agripa in 44 AD[13].

Thus comes the story of the mysterious monument of Kidron Valley, the Jerusalem Necropolis and the realm of the dead, to its temporary end. Who knows what knowledge research will bring us in the future, However, one important question remains to be answered. Since the 1950s, scholars have known beyond any doubt that despite the centuries old tradition, the monument is definitely not Absalom's Tomb. So, why is it that in all the books, maps and research papers and even on the explanatory sign placed near the monument itself, the name remains "The Tomb of Absalom"?

It's to teach every person who travels to Jerusalem a very important lesson. In a city that contains so many ancient stories, holy places and traditions, we never ever mess-up a good story with the facts.

---

[13] Barkai, G. (2016). *Yad Absalom - The Tomb of Herod Agripa King of Judah.* Researches of The City of David. Jerusalem.

SECRET ISRAEL

SECRET ISRAEL

THE FIRST ZIONIST

OLD CITY

N

The First Zionist

Rabbi Avraham Shlomo Zalman Tzoref Solomon, who due to his many names was commonly and more shortly known as Rashaz, was slowly but nervously pacing back and forth.

His shoes brushed against the expensive Persian carpets in the giant waiting-hall of Muhamad Ali's palace in Alexandria. Every few seconds he turned his eyes to the doors leading to the main hall, where he would soon meet with Muhamad Ali, the greatest ruler Egypt had known in the past few centuries. He arrived at the meeting too early on purpose, planning on having enough time to go over his strategy for the meeting in his head, and praying to God to assist him in his quest.

This was not Rashaz's first meeting with a man of Muhamad Ali's caliber and nervousness wasn't an emotion he dealt with very often. Other gushing emotions were definitely an inseparable part of his personality, and he controlled them with a fierce hand.

Rashaz often allowed himself to enjoy exhilaration and excitement when adventure was lurking ahead. He knew how to channel fear and convert it to bravery in the face of conflict or danger. He was an expert in reading people and confrontations, and knew exactly how to aim, pounce and land precisely on the thin line between opportunity and destruction. He was known for being sharp, resourceful and fearless.

Nevertheless, today, he was nervous.

When Rashaz left Jerusalem a month ago, he had assured everyone in his community of the Askenazi-Jews in Jerusalem beyond any doubt, that he would come back with the desired "Firman", an official document from the authorities acquitting them of all past debts and financial bindings to their Muslim creditors. However, as he was going over his plan in his head for the one hundredth time, he hoped everyone in Jerusalem was praying with extra devotion for him today.

What a long and tiring journey it has been, Rashaz pondered as he brushed his large calloused hand over his long beard over and over again. He still remembered it like it was yesterday, even though more than twenty years had passed since then, how he had to disguise himself with the robes and 'looks' of a Sephardic Jew in order to fool the guards at the gates and enter Jerusalem for the very first time in his life. All the Jews in the city of Tzfat thought he had lost his mind when he told them what he was about to do. 'They almost measured me for shrouds' he smiled to himself with satisfaction, realizing how his persistence, his perseverance and his faith in both God and man established a home for Ashkenazi Jews in Jerusalem after one hundred years of absence.

The words 'NO' or 'cannot', so it seemed, were always a temporary obstacle for Rashaz. A challenge you must solve. Never a final answer.

"It happened more than one hundred years ago", he was told by the elder Jews of Tzfat, in the Galilee mountains, when he first arrived from Lithuania, and learned that he and others like him were banned from ever setting foot in Jerusalem. "A group of Ashkenazi (Eastern-European) Jews came to Jerusalem in 1700 AD and borrowed money from the Muslim residents of the city, money they never managed to pay back. The debt was doubled and tripled time and time again, until paying it back became beyond reasonable reach. The debt kept rising until finally the Muslims creditors grew so furious that they banished the Ashkenazi Jews from Jerusalem. By 1720, Ashkenazi Jews were collectively banned from the city, and were held accountable, generation after generation, for the debt of their ancestors."

Rashaz listened intently but wasn't very impressed. He was a man of action and adventure, and he hadn't come all the way from Lithuania to the Holy Land, to never enter Jerusalem!

Moreover, Rashaz had a much higher cause at heart. He hadn't left his home and his parents just for himself. As a gifted teenager, he studied the preaching of the Gaon of Vilna[1], a Rabbi whose teachings revolutionized the face of the Jewish world in the beginning of the 19th Century. For hundreds of years, the  traditional diasporic Jewish view of redemption was passive, awaiting a miracle and conditioning the arrival of the Messiah by strict religious observance. This view was challenged by The Gaon of Vilna, who was viewed by his followers and scholars as a Godly messenger, put on earth to deliver a message of active redemption. According to his preaching and Kabalistic calculations, the Messiah was due to arrive at Jerusalem in the year 1840, and an active Jewish immigration to the Holy Land needed to take place in order for it to happen.

---

[1] Painting referred to the Gaon of Vilna. Source: Public Domain, Brockhaus and Efron Jewish Encyclopedia.

Even though the Gaon of Vilna himself never managed to complete his own journey to the Holy Land, he assembled many followers who transformed his preaching into a movement of active involvement of Jews worldwide in the construction of Jerusalem and the materialization of a self-sustained Jewish presence in it[2]. Rashaz was one of them. He still remembered the excitement that he held as a young man, no more than sixteen years old, when he realized that he, unlike his ancestors, wouldn't spend his life in the diaspora and pray for a miracle. He was about to embark on an adventure that only a handful of Jews took upon themselves in the past one thousand, seven hundred years - he was off to establish a prosperous Jewish presence in Jerusalem and prepare the city for the arrival of the Messiah.

At seventeen years of age, Rashaz married Chassia and took his wife and children and joined a group leaving Lithuania to the Holy Land. On the way, he broke off from the group and stayed in Istanbul to master a trade so he could make a living and support his family when they arrived in the Holy Land. Soon after, he became a goldsmith. This particular detail of his life may seem like an ordinary phase in the life of every young man, especially an immigrant who seeks to make a living in a new land, however, among Jews at that time, a Jew with a trade in the Holy Land (that wasn't part of the community services) was considered not only exceptional, but rebellious!

After the destruction of the Second Temple, Jews soon disappeared from the Holy Land. However, in the second millennium, Jews started to trickle back into the Holy Land, bit by bit. The reason for the Jewish absence was both external and internal. Externally, different empires that ruled the land had

---

[2] Morgenstern, A. (2007). *The Return to Jerusalem: The Jewish Resettlement of Israel, 1800-1860*, Shalem Center, Jerusalem. Pp. 3.

different views about the Jewish presence in the Holy Land and the rights or restrictions they were given.

Massacres of the Jewish community in the country were not rare throughout the history of the country either. Additionally, despite the constant presence of a Jewish community in the Holy Land throughout the generations, Jews worldwide deliberately avoided active attempts of settlement as a Jewish collective. The general assumption among the different Jewish communities was that the destruction of the Temple and life in exile were a punishment from God. The Jews therefore, must obey and await God to redeem them from their misery. This concept made the great Rabbis (with the exception of a small group of them throughout history) for centuries to forbid any collective attempt of settlement in the Holy Land. An attempt of that sort was considered sinful beyond imagination and could postpone redemption even further.

The Jewish presence in the Holy Land, not as an independent nation but as a small and often oppressed community, was viewed as crucial for the spiritual survival and development of Judaism worldwide. Jewish commentaries, religious laws and contemplations conceived in the Holy Land (and even better in Jerusalem itself) were considered to be of the highest degree. This was based on the Biblical verse:

> *"The law will go out from Zion, the word of the Lord from Jerusalem."*
>
> -   *Isaiah 2:3*

To ensure that the Jewish presence in Jerusalem was kept for the holy purpose of praying and Torah studying, the Jewish communities in the Holy Land often (not always, but for the most part) relied on the financial support of the Jewish communities in the diaspora, who were for the most part committed to contributing to this cause.

Rashaz arrived and discovered that the Jewish community in the Holy Land was almost completely relying on charity money collected among the Jewish communities in the diaspora, but he had no intention to take part in it. Instead, he was determined to change it, and thus improve the unstable financial condition of the Jewish community in Jerusalem. By doing so, he would make it attractive for more and more Jews to arrive and join the effort to build the city and prepare it for the arrival of the Messiah.

"The ones who are crazy enough to think they can change the world, are the ones that do," Steve Jobs said. Centuries earlier, Rashaz proved it to be true.

Rashaz truly believed that redemption could not come on its own. In other words, God helps those who help themselves. *"If there is no flour, there is no Torah"[3],* he knew. Despite the Jerusalem community's constant occupation in studying the Torah, in order to bring redemption, he knew he must change the way the system works, and to change the system, you must be a part of it.

"Oh, how far we've come", Rashaz thought, remembering how in the beginning, it was just him and a handful of Ashkenazi Jews, just enough to complete a Minyan (a Jewish praying group of ten men), and his single goldsmith workshop he opened among the Arab merchants in the Shook (the market). Despite his Lithuanian origin, he quickly managed to read, write and speak in Arabic, and thus to communicate not only with his Muslim neighbors, but with the official Ottoman authorities. After tedious efforts, countless attempts, and a lot of money finding its way to the right pockets, permission to return to Jerusalem was granted to the Ashkenazi

---

[3] Ethics of the Fathers, 3:21 מסכת אבות, פרק ג' משנה י"ז

Jews. The Ashkenazi neighborhood was ruined, trashed and rickety, but at least they were there, and that alone was a good enough reason to rejoice.

After the return to the city, Rashaz had a few immediate goals in mind - renovate the houses, renovate the old synagogue, and redeem "The Ashkenazi Courtyard", a part of the neighborhood that once belonged to the Ashkenazi community, but now was bare and forbidden. After the debt from 120 years ago, the debt owners and their heirs after them had decided to claim the land in place of the unpaid debt, opened eleven shops in this area and refused to leave. However, Rashaz knew this land's status as an "Ashkenazi Waqf", a charitable endowment of land under the Muslim law, dedicated for eternity to the Jewish Ashkenazi community, and therefore couldn't be claimed to pay a debt.

Despite the theoretical justice, his countless appeals to the Ottoman authorities seemed to be in vain. The cause seemed hopeless, until one day, the sound of 40,000 horseshoes were heard galloping towards the city gates, bringing with them the sound of changing times.

The sound of a door opening behind him woke Rashaz from his day-dream. The Austrian Consul to Egypt walked in with his usual frozen expression of a pompous filled with self importance.

"Ready for the meeting?" the consul asked.

"I hope he's as ready as I am?" Rashaz responded with a query.

"As we agreed," the consul answered. A hint of relief snuck up Rashaz's throat when he heard the consul's answer, helping him take slightly deeper breaths.

"How did you find him?" Rashaz asked.

"Intrigued, most certainly intrigued. Ali has great plans for the development of Egypt. He wants to make it into the France of the Middle East, minus this ghastly weather that is," the consul chuckled with satisfaction at his own joke. "Your connections with the Baron of Rothschild are definitely attractive in Ali's eyes.

'As they are in yours,' Rashaz thought but kept it to himself. Instead, he nodded with gratitude.

"You and Rothschild are close, ya?" the consul smiled and shook his head at him as he said "You Jews always stick together."

"We always stick together," Rashaz repeated the consul's words as confirmation.

"Und our agreement?" The consul asked

"Worry not Herr Consul. I will make sure Rothschild glorifies your name in the ears of the Austrian Emperor. Your promotion is only a matter of how quickly Egyptian pigeons can fly."

"With all due respect Rabbi, an important message such as this should be carried by an emissary!"

"Joke, my good man," Rashaz said. "Ein kleiner witz, to lighten the tension."

"Oh", the Austrian consul chuckled and snorted with laughter "Egyptian pigeon, wunderbar!" the consul shook Rashaz's hand. "Well, my good man, I will leave you to it then. Good luck!" he said and turned away.

Rashaz was relieved to see him leave. As he was walking, he could still hear the consul snorting and mumbling to himself "Egyptian pigeons... wunderbar..."

It seemed Rashaz's strategy was working, at least at first. He was hoping that the consul was right, and that Muhamad Ali was indeed interested in connections with the Rothschilds.

In the inner pocket of his coat, in a special compartment his wife Chassia sewed, were documents proving that the Ashkenazi Courtyard in Jerusalem was the property of the Ashkenazi community and is considered a Waqf, and a copper plate. He pressed the plate against his ribs with his forearm and decided to spend the time left until the meeting with prayers. Rashaz took out a book of Psalms from his other pocket and started davening intently while pressing the copper plate even tighter to his body. As he was reading through the old familiar words he already knew by heart, he remembered the day the copper plate was given to him, and hoped that the promise it was given with would finally be fulfilled.

Five years ago in 1831, Ibrahim Pasha, Muhamad Ali's son, left Egypt and went on a journey to conquer Syria from the Ottoman empire. On his way north to Damascus, he arrived at the gates of Jerusalem with forty thousand soldiers. Rashaz arrived in Jerusalem from Lithuania as an adult in 1811. Despite his foreign background and religion of minority, twenty years later he was already fluent in Arabic and was friendly with key figures of the Muslim quarter in Jerusalem. He knew very well that the presence of Ibrahim Pasha outside the walls was not a welcome sight.

The arrival of the army caused an uproar. Men locked their shops and ran home to safeguard their wives, women ran from their homes to the streets to find and protect their children, and children ran from the streets to the city's wall to catch a better view of the action.

Rashaz was sitting in the Kollel[4] studying when the door suddenly slammed open and someone yelled,

"The Egyptians are coming! The Egyptians are coming!"

Books fell to the floor, chairs were knocked over, and everyone ran outside. Rashaz waited for the room to clear, quickly blew out all the oil lamps, locked the door behind him, and ran quickly to the agreed meeting spot. When he arrived, he saw Miriam, his youngest daughter, running towards him, holding on to her long heavy skirt.

"Tatte! Tatte![5] The Egyptians are coming!" she yelled.

Whenever something happened, the Solomon family had an agreement - whomever isn't in the house will run to the agreed upon spot, and from there, they will run to the house together. This promise meant they would find one another quickly, instead of running all over the city to search for each other.

"Is Mamme[6] home?" Rashaz asked her as he grabbed her hand and they started running through the alley towards the house.

"I don't know", Miriam answered.

"What did you see? It's important you tell me", he asked. He knew her too well. Sometimes, Miriam had the feeling that her dad was a little bit like God, *"testing reins and heart."*[7]

---

[4] Advanced judaic studies center for men

[5] "Dad" in Yiddish

[6] Mom in Yiddish

[7] Jeremiah 11:20

"Ok, but don't tell Mamme," she said.

"Which wall did you climb this time?" Rashaz asked.

"The south. I saw the Egyptians marching, Tatte. Like a river of people, and they were riding horses and carrying big swords".

"Did Mamme bake anything today?" Rashaz asked.

"What?" Miriam asked. "Tatte are you feeling ok?"

"Never better. Did Mamme bake anything today?" He asked again.

"Honey cake I think." She said.

"Excellent. Miriam, when we get home, I want you to pour milk into my travel waterskin, then you and Mamme start cooking dinner as if it was Shabbos[8]!"

"Tatte, you are not going out there!" She couldn't hide her concern.

"Mirrelle[9] Don't worry, you're about to see how your mother's honey cake will save Jerusalem. *'For Zion's sake I will not keep silent'[10]* and *'God will keep us from all harm'[11]*."

Miriam knew that when her father started speaking in verses there was no use arguing. Her father 's tendency to always run head-first into danger drove her and Mother crazy, but she knew he had good instincts and learned to trust him. Still, the idea of Tatte going out

---

[8] Shabbat, Saturday, the holy day of the week for Jews

[9] Short for Miriam

[10] Isaiah 62:1

[11] Psalms 121:7

of the city walls to stand alone in front of the Egyptian army, armed with a cake, was to say the least, unpleasant.

Chassia, Rashaz's wife was holding the door open and watching the street with worry. When she saw her husband and daughter running towards her, she felt relieved. "What is going on?" she asked.

"They're here" her husband said while storming into the kitchen, "where's the honey cake?"

"In the pantry," Chassia said. "Who's here? And what do you want with the honey cake? I am not giving you a single piece until you tell me what is going on."

Rashaz took off his black coat and rushed to the water bowl to wash his hands and his face. "Mirrelle get me the Shabbos coat! And the good hat!" He said as he soaked his face and beard full of water.

"Yes Tatte!" Miriam ran to the closet.

"Chesselle, listen to me," he turned to his wife who seemed startled, confused and angry, all at the same time. "The Egyptian army is marching at the gates. They are probably led by Ibrahim Pasha, he is Muhamad Ali's son, and more importantly, he has never lost a battle. The Ottomans fear him. The Europeans fear him, everyone is fearing him!"

"Everyone but my husband" she replied, not liking where this was going.

"For twenty years we've been here, Chassia. Twenty long years and we are no closer to getting permission to renovate our synagogues or get back the Courtyard of the Ashkenazi than we were when we got here."

His daughter came back wearing his hat on her head and he smiled at her. She held his jacket for him to wear and he kept explaining while grabbing the hat off her head and tucking his shirt in his pants.

"In nine years, Messiah will be coming, and what will we tell him? That we were too afraid to redeem the land for him? Muhamad Ali is an enlightened ruler, he's stronger than the Ottomans and if he's marching through here, it means he is threatening the Sultan in Istanbul. Trust me, we want to be on his good side. I know you're worried, but trust me, this is a blessing. *"Israel is to be saved from Egypt."*[12]

"Shoyn shoyn,"[13] she said annoyed. "And now what? You're going to meet the Egyptian general at the gate and invite him over for dinner?" she asked sarcastically.

"*'A wife of noble character who can find'*[14]!" Rashaz quoted the famous verse from proverbs to his wife. "I don't even need to speak for you to understand, my sheine[15] Chesselle!" he grabbed her face to give her a big kiss while soaking her entire face in his wet beard. Then he snatched the honey cake Miriam wrapped and a waterskin full of milk from his daughter's hands, kissed her on top of her head and quickly headed to the door. "Cook for about ten people, maybe more, we'll be back in time for dinner!"

---

[12] Tanhuma (Aggadic Midrash in Rabbinical Literature) Exodus Parashah, Mark (siman) 17.

[13] "Fine" in Yiddish

[14] Every Friday night at the Kiddush (the Jewish ceremony separating between Shabbat and the rest of the week days) the husband is singing this quote from Proverbs 31:10 (NIV) to his wife, all the way to Proverbs 31:31.

[15] Pretty in Yiddish

"I want this to be a joke Avraham!" Chassia yelled from the threshold while wagging her finger at him.

"We'll laugh about it someday I promise! See you for supper!" he yelled without looking back as he was running down the street, towards the city's gate, leaving his wife to cool off and put together a good meal. "Thank you, God, for sending me a wife whose cooking will bring us redemption," he mumbled to himself as he approached the gate. There were three things he believed in with all his being in this life: God, the arrival of the Messiah, and Chassia's cooking.

Since the 4th Century AD, Jerusalem fell into the hands of many covetous rulers and generals, Christians and Muslims alike. Throughout the generations, some Jewish presence always existed in the city, and every time a new conqueror arrived at the gates - it was always a fateful question: What will become of the Jews? Will they be spared or massacred? History teaches unfortunately, that it was always a fifty-fifty chance. In that case, the obvious question is, what causes a Jewish Rabbi to believe his wife's cooking will save the Jews from being hurt by the approaching army?

Jerusalem, he knew, would fall into Ibrahim Pasha's hands without a fight, if the small guard the Ottomans delegated with protecting the city were smart enough to surrender and hope for mercy. Even if they wouldn't, the battle would be short. Ibrahim Pasha wouldn't be killed by sword, but this didn't mean there weren't thousands in the city who would scheme to poison him and bring his head to the Sultan at the Sublime Porte. Anyone who'd manage that would be rewarded beyond his wildest dreams.

With his wife's cooking as his protective shield, Rashaz marched towards the Egyptian army, and was escorted by guards to the tent of General Ibrahim Pasha.

"A Salam Aleikum![16]" Rashaz greeted General Pasha as he entered the tent.

"WaAleikum A Salam" the general greeted in return.

Ibrahim Pasha, by Giovanni Boggi, 19th Century. [17]

Rashaz began speaking in perfect Arabic and made it clear just how welcome General Pasha is by the Jews of the city.

"The Jews of the city are at your service," he said, "and I will make sure to provide you with any need, big or small. We are relieved with your arrival and want to make sure we do everything we can to assist Muhamad Ali in occupying Ballad A Sham[18] and

---

[16] "Peace be upon you", a common welcome greeting in Arabic.

[17] Source: Public Domain, 1850+

[18] The Arabic name describing the area of Syria and the land of Israel, commonly used during the time of the Ottoman empire.

take his rightful place as the ruler of Jerusalem. Under the Ottoman regime Jews are backsliding. The empire is dying, but we don't want to die with it. In Europe however, Jews are thriving and they are a crucial part in the financial and technological growth. Allow us to join you, and we will do our part to contribute to your prosperity."

Rashaz felt this was a good time to stop and "check the room." This could end with the Jewish community being spared, or with his head being chopped off right there on the spot. The swords the guards were carrying definitely looked sharp enough to make it quick. He looked Ibrahim Pasha straight in the eye, to establish a connection of trust. General Pasha looked back at him and seemed pleased.

"Go on", he said.

"Many in the city would like to help you die, so they can bring your head as a gift to the Sublime Porte. Your head won't leave your shoulders in a battle here. Of that I am sure. I heard of your record. You are probably the most capable warrior who marched into this land since Baibars the Mamluk, Rashaz said. "While you're here though, you will need to rely on our stocks for food and supplies, and this is where I am worried for your safety. As a personal gesture of trust from our community, we would like to invite you to dine at our table for as long as you're here."

Rashaz then knelt and opened his bundle on the ground. He revealed the honey cake, broke a piece off of it, and ate. Then he opened the waterskin and drank while making the gulping and swallowing sound loud and clear. He then stepped back as the guards handed General Pasha the food and the drink. The general ordered his men to serve coffee and he and Rashaz sat together and discussed many different matters.

So it was that for the time General Ibrahim Pasha stayed in Jerusalem, Chassia and Miriam worked at the kitchen for hours each day, and Rashaz delivered the food to the General's residence personally. Soon enough, General Pasha established his rule and placed a guard of his own in Jerusalem, and the time came to march with the army north, towards Syria. That evening, the General summoned Rashaz to his tent, to thank him, and to say goodbye. When Rashaz arrived, Ibrahim granted him a copper plate, and said:

> *"You are very welcome in my eyes and deserve a reward for the warm hospitality you showed me. Today, I have no gift to give you and in my hand is nothing but a copper plate. I am giving you the plate as a sign and a memory. Any time you would like to come and meet with me or with Muhamad Ali, show the plate to the guards, and you will be welcome without delay."*[19]

Five years have passed since then. Rashaz gave up on concentrating on the prayer, kissed the book of Psalms and placed it back in his pocket. Five years of countless letters, requests and attempts to promote the community's needs, and nothing. Years went by, many good and blessed reforms happened in the land under the short rule of Muhamad Ali. Rashaz was more than pleased with the progress, but building the new synagogue and getting back the Ashkenazi Courtyard didn't progress an inch, and it drove him mad, like an itch he could not scratch.

Finally, the door opened, and he walked into the great hall to meet with the great Muhamad Ali, face to face.

---

[19] Mendelboim S. (2014). *The Figure and Actions of Avraham Shlomo Zalman Tzoref - HaRashaz*. Beit Solomon - Three Generations to the Founder of the Yeshuv. Zalman Shazar. Jerusalem. Pp. 25.

Muhamad Ali, by Auguste Couder, 19ᵗʰ Century. [20]

Rashaz followed his plan and everything went even smoother than he could have possibly hoped for. Muhamad Ali recognized his son's copper plate and thanked Rashaz for the loyalty he demonstrated in the conquering of Jerusalem.

---

[20] Source: Public Domain. Auguste Couder, 19th Century.

A few years after Jerusalem moved into Egyptian hands, a rebellion was stirred up by the local farmers, who protested against Ali's demand to recruit young men for his military.

"You must understand how difficult this is," Ali said. "Their productivity is extremely low. These farmers are more productive as soldiers on the battlefield than they are as farmers paying low taxes. Religion aside, I've seen the European troops. We are centuries behind them with our fighting abilities. This society needs to become productive and educated in order to prosper, but these things don't happen overnight. Right now I need to improve my forces. For now, it's just the farmers, but the Sublime Porte won't remain still for much longer. The Sultan is finished, and when the time comes, I want Europe to understand that Egypt under my control is the riding power of modernity in the Middle East. A military needs money like a fish needs water."

Rashaz nodded with understanding and replied, "We share the same lack of affection to the Sublime Porte. For years they have been agreeing with me that the Courtyard in Jerusalem is a Jewish Waqf, belonging to the Ashkenazi community of Jerusalem by right, but when it is time to take action, the officials' pockets swallow money like a bottomless pit, and we get nothing in return. Your son told me how you were promised the island of Crete as a reward for your help with the fight against the Greeks. Did they deliver? Of course not. You and I are both men of action who want to bring modernity and prosperity to the land. Redeem it from its miserable barrenness. So is the Baron of Rothschild. There is nothing this old man would like to see more than the Jews return to their rightful place in Jerusalem and help it prosper with a booming economy, like Jews are doing everywhere in Europe. That's why he is so generous with our communities. Your help to the cause, should it be given, will be of the highest value to the Baron, and in return, I'm sure he'll reward you."

Muhamad Ali seemed pleased. He called on one of his viziers to come closer and whispered something in his ear. The vizier then left in a hurry.

"Very well," Muhamad Ali said. "I've heard enough. The court of the Ashkenazi in Jerusalem is yours. By the time you leave Egypt my men will make sure you hold the official Firman for it. You make sure to tell your friend the Baron that you did not leave Muhamad Ali's palace empty handed, and that the Jews are welcome and safe under my rule."

Rashaz thanked Muhamad Ali from the bottom of his heart and left the palace. He was then accompanied to an office where the fresh Firman was being copied and signed. The document was placed in his hand and he tucked it deep into the inner pocket of his travel coat, next to his Siddur[21].

At last, Rashaz walked out of Muhamad Ali's palace and was getting ready to return home with his promise to the community fulfilled. He rushed towards the inn he was staying in, but not before passing by the Austrian consulate to shake the hand of his pompous friend, and thank him kindly for his help. Rashaz had a few letters to write and was hoping to make it to the post office before closing time. As he walked along the coast of Alexandria, he inhaled the fresh salty air of the Mediterranean and felt as if a boulder was lifted off of his chest.

"Now", he thought in his heart, "all that's left is to write to the Baron of Rothschild, introduce myself, hope he would like to be my friend, and perhaps start our friendship by funding the reconstruction of the Ashkenazi quarter in Jerusalem..."

---

[21] A Jewish prayer book.

The story about Rashaz doesn't end there. The money donated to the Jews in the Holy Land was all channeled and divided through a single Jewish organization in Amsterdam.

They decided which Kollel and which congregation got money, and how much of it. The head of this organization, Hirsh Lehren, wasn't a fan of Rashaz's, to say the least. Lehren believed that Jews in Jerusalem must devote themselves entirely to studying the Torah in order to bring redemption. Therefore, they must be funded and depend on donations from Jews around the world. Rashaz's vision to establish a self-sustaining community and an independent Jewish economy in Jerusalem, seemed extremely dangerous in Lehren's eyes, not to mention that it created some very unwelcome competition in the diaspora-fundraising field.

As soon as Rashaz arrived at the inn, he grabbed a paper and a quill, and sat down to write three letters. One to his family, informing them that he had accomplished his goal, and was headed back to Jerusalem. The second, to the one authority that until then approved the foreign funding of anything in the Holy Land, the Jewish Administrative Organization in Amsterdam. Rashaz wrote to Mr. Lehren, informing him about his actions in Egypt, and kindly requested Lehren to raise the necessary donations from the Baron of Rothschild. He tucked the letter into the envelope, fully aware that Lehren was about to lose his temper and deny his request without giving it a second thought. Therefore, the third letter he wrote was addressed directly to the Baron of Rothschild.

In the letter Rashaz described his vision to rebuild the Jewish presence in Jerusalem. He told him of the ruined synagogue which had been standing like a pile of rocks, filled with garbage for centuries, due to the Ottoman law that forbade Jews and Christians from renovating their houses of prayer. He told him about his fruitful efforts with Muhamad Ali and kindly requested a donation for the renovation of the synagogue and the reconstruction of the Ashkenazi Courtyard.

There is no way for me to prove this, but if I had to guess, I'd say the letter to Rothschild was probably deposited in the loyal hands of the best emissary Rashaz could find, and the letter to Hirsh Lehren was probably delivered by an Egyptian Pigeon.

Rashaz, apparently, was right. After his return to Jerusalem, a letter from Lehren arrived soon enough, in which he declared that he declined Rashaz request for funding, and that he hadn't the slightest intention to even mention any of this, in the ears of the Baron of Rothschild. Luckily, by the time Lehren's letter arrived in Jerusalem, Rashaz already received the letter from the Baron of Rothschild himself, complimenting him on his vision and actions, and declaring that the Baron will be delighted to donate his money for the reconstruction of the Ashkenazi Courtyard, and the synagogue inside it.

Despite the predictions and the hard work, the year 1840 came and went, and the Messiah did not come. Rashaz's efforts to keep constructing Jerusalem never stopped. Within a few years, the descendants of the debt owners left the courtyard (not without a fight) which wasn't theirs to begin with, the community pulled together, and with the Baron's money, it only took a few years for the neighborhood to grow and prosper. Even After Muhamad Ali was forced by the European superpowers to leave the Holy Land and give the land back to the Ottomans, the Jews were allowed to keep their land and their new structures.

However, not everyone was happy with the outcome. The descendants of the debt owners, the same debt from 130 years ago, were furious for being forced to leave the quarter, and decided to kill the person who was responsible for their loss.

One morning, Rashaz was walking down the alley on his way to his morning prayer, when suddenly, a few Muslims snuck up on him from behind and knocked him out with a sword blow to his head. The head blow caused him to lose his memory, and for several months he laid in his bed, mumbling meaningless words. Finally, on September 16, 1851, his consciousness suddenly returned to him. He requested his family members to assemble around his bed, blessed each one of his children, and commanded them to never leave the Holy Land. Then, he prayed the "Shema"[22] and returned his soul to the creator. He was 65 years old.

Like many righteous men in Jerusalem, Rashaz was buried in the foothills of the Mount of Olives, where he would be able to witness the Messiah when he does come, firsthand.

The story didn't end there. Even after his death, Rashaz's tomb was often vandalized by Musllims who held grudges against him for taking back the neighborhood. Finally, his descendants decided to move his tomb and hide it, placing it away from wicked eyes, so that his rest won't be bothered anymore.

***

"And where is it hidden?" I asked my dad.

"I don't know exactly", My dad said. "But it says here it is in the Mount of Olives".

I was young then. No more than ten years-old. I was interested in my family's roots. When I asked my dad where did our family come from, he told me that Grandma survived the Holocaust in

---

[22] A Jewish prayer Jews pray every day. Also the prayer a person says if they know they are about to die. The prayer is said in Hebrew and is a citation from the Old Testament, Deuteronomy 6:4.

Russia and that grandpa's family had been in this country for many generations. "How many?" I asked.

"Well, let's see," my dad got up and pulled a fancy looking book with a navy cover and golden letters off of the bookshelf. The cover said:

"Ten Generations in the Land of Israel - The Family of Rabbi Avraham Shlomo Zalman Tzoref Solomon."

"That's a lot of names for one person!" I declared and my father laughed.

At the time I was young, but old enough to understand that this wasn't something ordinary. I knew the general history of my people in this land and the narrative was well known and established. The Jews came to Israel as part of the Zionist movement at the end of the 19th Century, to escape antisemitism and materialize their aspirations for an autonomous Jewish homeland. Most of the Jews arrived in Israel either right before World War II or right after it, when the state of Israel was established. In my generation, those born in the 1980s, it meant that for pretty much all of us, our parents, grandparents or at most great grandparents, immigrated to Israel from somewhere else. This meant four generations. And here sits my father, holding a book called "Ten Generations in the land of Israel."

"So this book is about some old ancestor of our family?" I asked.

"Not just the old ancestors", my father answered, "you as well".

"This book is about me?" I couldn't believe my ears.

"Yes", he said, "Our family is one of the most ancient families of Ashkenazi Jews in the land. This book was sent to me by members of the family who kept track and record of the generations."

My father flipped the pages of the book and his calloused finger traced over a long list of names on the pages. "Here is my name", he said, "and there you are, and your sister". "What about Aviv?", I asked about my youngest brother.

"I'm afraid this edition was published before he was born. He didn't make it to this one. He'll have to get in on the next edition."

Bummer, I thought, to be left out of the family book just because you were too late to be born. Still, I felt special. It's not every day a young girl sees her name in a book about important people.

My dad and I went over the book together and he told me the story, for as much as a ten- year-old can understand.

***

Years went by and I became a tour guide. Soon after, my father passed away. Even after all of these years of knowing about this story, I still didn't know where exactly Rashaz was buried, until one day, I guided a tour for my friend Yiftah's family. Yiftah is Israeli, he and I went to pre-military training together, and his family has been up and down and all around. Both his parents were Israeli born and raised, so he asked me to take them to see places that are special and off the beaten-path.

Naturally, I decided to take them down to the Kidron Valley's tombs. We started our visit in Absalom's Tomb, and from there walked south down the Kidron Valley, to the Tomb of Zechariah.

The Nefesh, Zechariah's Monument, 2009. [23]

"Much like the Tomb of Absalom," I started my guiding session. "This structure is a Monolith, carved from the rock surrounding it. However, unlike the Tomb of Absalom we've just visited, this entire structure is a Monolith. No part was carved and added, one rock from top to bottom. The structure is a block, the walls are decorated with ionic pilasters and on top - an Egyptian cornice. This structure is also a mix of Greek and Egyptian architecture, and is dated to the middle of the 2nd Century BC, the time of the 2nd Temple. Traditionally, throughout history, this tomb was known as the Tomb of Zechariah, but the question is, which Zechariah? How many Zechariahs do you know in our Biblical history?"

---

[23] Source: Pikiwiki photo stock, Credit: Yigal Zalmanson, 2009.

I looked straight to Yiftah, expecting him to come up with the answers. He was, after all, in an excellers program at the university to become a Tanakh (Old Testament) teacher, and that's regardless of his other helpful hobby: Trivia.

"Zechariah son of Jehoiada the high priest," he said as I expected. "He spoke against the sins of the people in the name of God and was stoned to death by the order of Jehoash, King of Judea[24]. But this can't be his tomb."

"That's incredibly accurate," I said. "And why not?"

"Because Zechariah, son of Jehoiada lived during the time of the first temple, and you said this tomb is dated for the second."

"What about Zechariah the prophet? Zechariah son of Berechiah? Wasn't he prophesying during the time of the 2nd temple?" Yiftah's dad, who was also a big Trivia fan, asked.

"You are both right and wrong," I said. "True, Zechariah the prophet is dated to have been alive during the time of the 2nd temple, but he lived during the 6th and the 5th centuries, and this tomb is dated for the 2nd. But you were really close!" I added, realizing that normal people don't walk around the land with the list of Bible characters and their dates memorized... I decided then to add the last option to the mix, "There is one more Zechariah we didn't mention, he was a priest in the 2nd Temple, and the father of John the Baptist from the New Testament."

"So is he the one who's buried here?" Yiftah asked.

"Sadly, no. You see, Zechariah was born in the 1st century BC and died in the 1st century AD, so I'm afraid it isn't him either".

---

[24] 2 Chronicles 24

"Maybe he was just somebody's uncle," Yiftah said. I looked up at the 60 feet tall monument, and we all laughed.

"Actually Yiftah, I can assure you that the person buried here wasn't anybody's uncle. In fact, he wasn't anybody's anything[25]. When archeologists started digging and examining this 'tomb' they realized that this monolithic monument remained sealed. There was never any opening carved, nor a grave inside. Archeologists found it very weird, however right above us, up the staircase on the north side of this monument, is the burial cave of the family of Hezir, one of the twenty-four priestly divisions who served in the temple. At the entrance to the burial cave, there is an inscription in Hebrew:

This is the grave and the Nefesh... of Benei (sons of) Hania,
Kohanim (priests) of the Hezir family.

"Nefesh, as you all know, is the Hebrew word for 'soul', but in ancient times, it was also a word to describe a monument in memory of someone who died. This is a fascinating concept, considering when this *Nefesh* was built. The family of Hezir who's buried right above, as well as all the 'Zechariahs' that are suggested to have been buried here, were priests in the 1st or 2nd Temple. The priests in the time of the 2nd Temple were Sadducees, a conservative and rich sect of Jewish society who worked at the Temple and had a lot of power over the Jews of the

---

[25] There is an assumption in research suggested by Prof. Adiel Schremer, that the monument is actually the tomb of Uzziah king of Judea. The assumption is based on two written documents, one from the 12th century and one from 1810. In addition, it is based on "The Inscription of Uzziah" presented in the Israel Museum, after it was removed from its original spot. Therefore, though the assumption does have some base to it, it is currently under the definition of an "assumption" only. For this reason, I did not elaborate about it in this book, however it was important for me to bring comprehensive and up to date information in this book, for the more inquisitive reader.
Schremer, A. (1987). *More About Uzziah's Tomb*. Katedra Periodical. Yad Yizhak Ben Zvi, Jerusalem.

time. They opposed the other sect of Judaism, the Pharisees, whose ideas were more spiritual and Messianic. These two sects were divided over many ideological, social and religious topics. One of the biggest divisions was about the concept of the afterlife. The Sadducees, who were also very rich, denied any claim for an afterlife. They followed the written Torah, materialism, and revoked prophecies and faith in angels. They claimed the reward or punishment for your deeds, are given to you in this world."

The burial cave of Hezir (left), next to the Nefesh, before excavation, 1934. [26]

"But they didn't survive the destruction of Jerusalem and the Temple," Yiftah said.

"True," I continued. "When the Temple was destroyed, so were the Sadducees. The Material of the Temple and Jerusalem was gone, and so were they. The Pharisees however, managed to convert Judaism to a spiritual idea, one that can also exist outside the borders of the Holy Land. We, the Jews who survived generation after generation for two thousand years, are the

---

[26] Source: Pikiwiki photo stock, Credit: Hanse Loyrer, 1934. Negative Scan by Yonatan Loyrer.

descendants of the Pharisees, and they believed in the eternity of the soul, of the *Nefesh*."

"Fascinating!" Yiftah said, then he quoted a known Hebrew expression from the Talmud:

"You don't build Nefashot (monuments) for the righteous. Their words and actions are their commemoration."[27]

"Exactly!" I said with excitement, "It is very possible my friends, that we are a group of the Pharisees' descendants, gazing at a Sadducee *Nefesh*. A Sadducee concept of commemorating the dead.

"I don't believe you!" Yiftah said with an over-acted expression of seriousness. I knew he was joking. "Archeology shmarcheology, they just didn't know how to look! I'm going to show you this is no *Nefesh*, I'll find a way in!" he said and with his hand held high and playing like he was on a mission, he ran, climbed over the rocks and disappeared behind the giant monument.

"Yiftah!" I yelled, laughing at the same time with the rest of his family.

"Well, what do we do now?" I asked the rest of the family who was left behind.

"We can go. He's a goner," his girlfriend Aviv said laughing.

"Alright then", I said amused, when finally, I heard Yiftah's voice calling me from behind the monument.

---

[27] Jerusalem Talmud, Shkalim Tractate, Chapter 2 Halacha 5

"Shakked! Shakked come over here, there is something behind here!"

"If I don't come back in 5 minutes, please make sure my tomb says this was Yiftah's fault," I said. His family stayed back, and I climbed the rocks expecting to be pranked at any moment, but I was wrong.

Yiftah stood behind in the gap between the giant monument and the rock of the mount of Olives, next to two relatively "new-looking" graves. "Did you know about this?" he asked.

"No, I never climbed up here," I said. I walked closer to read the words on the tombs and couldn't believe my eyes. The one tomb said:

"The Burial Place of Avraham Shlomo Zalman, may his righteous memory be a blessing, who saved the Ashkenazi Courtyard from the hands of the Ishmaelites, and put effort into building the synagogue of Menachem Zion. Died on Sept. 16th, 1851."

Shakked, paying a visit to the tomb of Rashaz, 2020. [28]

---

[28] Credit: Maya Shipelski, 2020. Personal Collection.

Next to his tomb was the tomb of his wife, Chassia.

"This doesn't look like a tombstone from 1851" Yiftah said.

"No, it isn't", I said. "This is the tomb of the founding father of my family, who brought the Ashkenazi Jews back to Jerusalem. I knew he was buried in the Mount of Olives, and our family moved his tomb to where it won't be vandalized anymore".

"Did you know it was here?" Yiftah asked, astonished.

"No," I answered. "But now, thanks to you, I do," I said, feeling the tears coming up my throat.

"You don't build monuments for the righteous," Yiftah said and put his arm on my shoulder. *"Their words and actions are their commemoration."*

"A *Nefesh* behind a *Nefesh*," I said and smiled. A soul behind a monument.

Yiftah gave me a hug and then went back to tell everyone about the magnitude of his finding, about a blessed, silly behavior that brought me closer to my roots than ever before, and left me in solitude with the tombs.

I thought about all that this person did and went through to bring the Jews back to Jerusalem. All that he kept doing even after the hope to see the Messiah in his life never came true. I realized that his vision and actions were the reason that I, and many others, are Jews living in the Holy Land independently, masters of our own fate.

It struck me all of a sudden that he did all of that decades before 'Zionism' even began to bud, in 1881. He must have been brave, bold and fearless. It takes a person with strong faith and vision to see in your spirit something that doesn't exist, and then make it a reality. A wave of gratitude flooded me. I inhaled a deep breath of the Jerusalem air and said to the tomb, "Thank you, Rashaz, for everything you did and for everything we are because of you. I promise to be back. Oh, and sorry you never got to see the Messiah in your day. Don't worry, we'll keep waiting.

"

THE SMALL WESTERN WALL

OLD CITY

N

The Small Western Wall

When I was sixteen, I used to ditch school quite often to go on day trips to explore the country. This is not an easy confession to make, as I'm sure that my mom, who's my biggest fan, is probably reading this, and she was the main authority I needed to avoid (sorry mom…).

Back then I was already very adventurous, and a school day just didn't cut it. Given that my tests and papers were always graded high (except math, which I was promised is extremely important but oddly, my guiding career never brought an equation with two variables my way), I preferred to spend my days exploring and collecting memories.

In my mom's defense, she would drop me off at school every morning. It wasn't her fault that as soon as she'd drive to work, I would climb over the fence and leave to the central bus station.

One of my favorite destinations (the thought of how reckless I was back then scares me today), was the old city of Jerusalem.

A walk through the alleyways of the old city of Jerusalem is both adventurous and dangerous. Despite the city being no bigger than 0.4 square miles, the quarters are very different from one another.

Jordanian Soldier standing on ruins of a Synagogue, holding a Torah scroll, 1948[1]

The Jewish Quarter for instance, is all "new and shining," because after the war in 1948, the Jews of the old city were taken captive to Jordan and their houses were destroyed. After the war, the Jews were returned to Israel, but the old city was in Jordanian territory. Why did the Jordanians destroy the Jewish Quarter? Such is war. One of the customs was to destroy the enemy's property, so they can never have it back. After the Six-Day War in 1967, the Jordanians retreated behind the Jordan River, and Jerusalem and the Temple Mount, after more than two thousand years, were once again in Jewish hands.

When the Jews returned to their quarter, no house remained standing. Everything was either excavated or rebuilt. Those who walk around the old city will easily recognize the Jewish Quarter, since almost every stone there was either built or excavated after 1967.

---

[1] Source: Public Domain. Credit: Arthur Derounian aka John Roy Carlson 1948.

Everywhere else in the city, with the exception of some newer churches, is made up of clusters of old buildings. Many date back to the Ottoman, or Mamluk period, and some are even older, from the time of the crusaders, which means they're almost a thousand years old.

The Armenian Quarter's proximity to the Jewish Quarter brings out its old age a little bit. Maybe because it is so clean and quiet, it gives visitors some time to take in the old age of the buildings. The quarter is nice and quiet and residential, and the Armenians keep to themselves for the most part. The houses are behind closed courtyards, and it's rare to see people hanging out in the streets. They are usually on their way to and from. The gates to these courtyards are decorated with signs of the family's name, usually with Armenian ceramic work decorated in red, white and blue, which is worldly famous and sold in the different shops in the Old City. The residents of the quarter are the "veterans" of the city, as the Armenians had already come to Jerusalem in the 4th Century AD. Some of them are survivors of the Armenian genocide done by the Ottomans in WWI, who escaped and found shelter with the Armenian community in Jerusalem.

Armenian Ceramics, 2010.[2]

---

[2] Source: Pikiwiki photo stock. Credit: Israel Preker, 2010

The Christian Quarter, like the Armenian one, shows signs of old age, but it is full of life. Monks, priests and nuns of all colors and uniforms walk in it. Nuns in white and gray robes and light blue head-covers. The Franciscan monks with their brown habits and rope-belt with three knots tied at its bottom, reminding them of their three vows: chastity, poverty, and obedience. The Coptic monks with their black garments and head covers decorated with thirteen crosses (representing Jesus and his twelve disciples). The Ethiopian monks and priests with their unique garments, and simple believers who come to the quarter to volunteer in the churches and serve them. All are different in their garments, colors and affiliation, but all are the same in the God they believe in. The Christian Quarter has its own unique smell too.

View of the Old City of Jerusalem, 2013[3]

The smell of incense comes out from the churches and travels the small and crowded streets. Sometimes I wonder if one day all the incense will be gone, would the smell be gone too, or is it already an inseparable part of the buildings and the pavement.

The market area sells an endless selection of Holy Land souvenirs, specifically Christian related, but not exclusively. Candles and incense sticks can be found in every corner, as well as crosses,

---

[3] Source: Pikiwiki photo stock. Credit: Lehava Center Nazarath, 2013.

rosaries and Nativity scenes carved from olive wood. Behind the market, though, the area is quiet and peaceful. In the quarter, there are hotels and coffee shops to attend to the many pilgrims, as well as over fifty churches of different denominations, and closed courtyards for the clergy. Some old and some new, The Christian population of the old city is zestful and active.

The Muslim Quarter is completely different, a world of its own. Not only is it the largest quarter of the city, it is also the most crowded one. While the population in the other three quarters put together doesn't exceed five thousand people[4], the Muslim quarter contains over thirty thousand residents. It is the only quarter inside the walls that kept its "Ancient-Middle-Eastern" appearance with the traditional open market, and ancient buildings.

The population is of a lower socioeconomic class, generally speaking, and due to internal politics of the different religious Muslim leaderships, the quarter has hardly been renovated, keeping its historical appearance. The quarter is usually crowded, filled with people of all colors, shapes and sizes. The market is colorful, loud and full of life, and when you go deeper into the neighborhood, the variety of smells is hard to ignore.

As a teenager going on my little 'adventures,' I tried staying on the main streets. I didn't have a map, and something told me that if I entered the tiny and twisting alleys, finding my way out wouldn't be as easy. I was right. The old city may be small, but getting lost in it is way easier than it should be. On my little day trips, I'd usually enter through Jaffa's gate, where the bus stopped, go through the market, sometimes arrive at the church of Holy Sepulcher, and wrap it up at the Western Wall.

---

[4] Municipality of Jerusalem. (2017). *Neighborhoods in Jerusalem.* The Official Website of the Municipality of Jerusalem.

Nearly everyone who visits Jerusalem visits the Western Wall, and even those who never visited Jerusalem heard about it. The most commonly known fact about the Western Wall is that it is the holiest place in the world for Jews. Like most of the commonly known facts about the most famous places in Israel, this fact is actually wrong.

Since the dawn of the Abrahamic presence in the Holy Land, the holiest place for the chosen people was Mount Moriah, later called the Temple Mount. According to most of the research, the First and the Second Temple both stood on that mountain. In its last reconstruction, a gigantic platform, like a stage, was built by King Herod the Great on top of the mountain. On top of the platform, he built the Second Temple, more magnificent than it ever was before. In fact, it was so glorious that even non-Jews used to come on a pilgrimage to the Holy Land to visit it and witness the wonder with their own eyes. The Second Temple stood on top of the platform until 70 AD, when the Jewish rebellion against the Romans was crushed, Jerusalem fell, and the Temple was destroyed.

Holy of Holies in the Second Temple, Israel Museum's Model, 2008 [5]

---

[5] Source: Attribution. Credit: Deror Avi, 2008.

After the destruction of the Temple, Jews were banned from Jerusalem for a few centuries. The temple itself, despite being the holiest place in the world for the Jews, never returned to its original function. Under the Roman Empire, 70 AD to 325 AD, it was converted into a paganistic temple. In the Byzantine Era, 325 AD to 638 AD, the first Christian era of the Holy Land, it became a garbage pile, to commemorate Jesus's prophecy of the destruction of the Temple. In the first and early Muslim period, 638 AD to 1099 AD, the Muslims who conquered the land cleaned the Temple Mount and built a mosque on top of it. Later on, they built the monumental structures of The Dome of the Rock and the Al-Aqsa Mosque.

The Dome of the Rock on the Temple Mount, estimated Temple's location, 2019.[6]

Traditionally, Islam recognizes this place as the location of Muhamad's ascension to heaven to recieve the holy chapters of the Quran. When the crusaders conquered the city, 1099 AD to 1293 AD, they converted the Dome of the Rock, which they recognized as the Second Temple, into a Christian shrine and the Al-Aqsa Mosque, which they recognized as the temple of King Solomon, into a palace for the kings of Jerusalem and later on, as

[6] Source: Pikiwiki photo stock. Credit: Lehava Center Nazarath, 2013.

the residence of the Templar Knights, who were known as "The Poor Fellow-Soldiers of Christ and of the Temple of Solomon." When the Crusaders lost the land to the Mamluks in 1293AD, the Temple Mount's structures took back their Muslim functions, and remain so to this day.

And the Jews? After the rebellion, they were banned from entering the city. In the Byzantine Era they were allowed to pay ransom money for permission to enter the city for the sole purpose of approaching the foothills of the platform, and crying over their long-gone temple.

Over the centuries, Jews were slowly allowed to return to Jerusalem, mainly under Muslim regimes. More often than not, they were not allowed to visit the mountain itself[7]. In order to pray and cry over the destruction of the temple, they assembled for prayer at the bottom of the western wall of the platform, the wall that was the closest to the Holy of Holies, the holiest and most important place of the temple. Next to this Western Wall, generations of Jews cried over the destruction of the temple and their nation's exile from the land. For this reason, the Western Wall is also commonly known as "The Wailing Wall."

When the state of Israel was established, Jerusalem was declared as its capital, but the old city, and the Western Wall inside it, remained in the hands of the Kingdom of Jordan. When Jerusalem was won during the Six-Day War in 1967, Israel Defense Force

---

[7] In Jewish literature and tradition there are Jewish sages and leaders that visited the Temple Mount over the centuries, such as Maimonides, and others. However, this tradition was not consistent, didn't include the majority of the people, and mainly depended on the agreement of the authorities of the time, which were rarer than not.

Parkash, T. Mendelbaum, E. (2016). *Not Just the Western Wall - The Forgotten and Holier Wall.* Ynet Judaism. Ynet.

soldiers headed first and foremost to the Temple Mount, the holiest place in the world for Jews since the time of Abraham.

However, due to its holiness to the Muslims, and the explosive sensitivity of the matter, the Temple Mount with its Muslim structures remained standing, and is still under Muslim control today, with the supervision of the Israeli domestic police force. Muslims alone are allowed to pray on the mountain and visit the structures. Non-Muslims, meaning Jews and Christians, are allowed to visit the mountain under very harsh restrictions. They aren't allowed to enter the Dome of the Rock or the Al-Aqsa Mosque, they aren't allowed to pray, bring a Bible with them, play music, sing or even close their eyes in prayer, or they risk being banned from the mountain by the religious Waqf police.

The Western Wall, 1967[8]

The State of Israel took a decision to leave the mountain as it was, to avoid a conflict with the entirety of the Muslim world. Under

---

[8] Source: Public Domain, 1967.

these circumstances, the area left for Jews to pray in and to call holy is the Western Wall, which has collected its own set of traditions and holy qualities over the centuries.

The closeness of the Western Wall to the Holy of Holies and the strong Jewish belief that prayers made at the wall will be fulfilled, made it into the holiest place in which Jews are allowed to pray and perform rituals. Well, sort of. If only things were that simple.

Jews may be only 0.2% of the world's population, but for such a tiny group, we are sure as divided as can be.

Common inside jokes, such as "in a room with two Jews there are eight opinions", or "in the state of Israel we have nine million citizens and nine million prime ministers", are too close to the truth. Not all Jews agree on what the best way to be a Jew is, and what the ultimate lifestyle is for Judaism. We are broadly divided into sects of Ultra-Orthodox, Orthodox, Modern Orthodox, Conservatives, Reformed, Reconstructionists, Traditional, Secular (ethnically Jewish), etc. Some of these sects are divided into even smaller subgroups and nuances. Unfortunately, the divisions between the groups are sometimes so harsh, they prevent us from being able to worship together.

In the case of the Western Wall for instance, divisions are harsh. Due to the lack of separation in Israel between religion and state, the Western Wall was given to the controlling Jewish authority in Israel, The Orthodox Rabbinical Establishment, which is known for its strict piety, and isn't close to making the Jewish majority in Israel or in the world. The Western Wall was officially recognized as a Jewish orthodox synagogue, which means different rules apply, such as modest dress codes, a complete separation between men and women, and prohibition on Jewish women to pray in a manner that is traditionally only for Jewish men.

Division between men and women section in the Western Wall, 2015.[9]

Still, with all the difficulties and the conflicts, the Western Wall is one of the most important places to visit in Israel, and a place no visitor in Jerusalem misses, given that it is public and open twenty-four hours a day.

When I used to take my little day tours outside of school, I'd often come to the Western Wall, or as we call it in Hebrew, the Kotel, and my feelings were always mixed. On one hand, I knew I was standing in a holy place, close to the Holy of Holies. However, I never liked crowded places, and the Kotel, unless you go there late at night, is almost always packed with people. Especially in the women's section which is significantly smaller than the men's section, even though there are almost always more women than men at the Kotel at any given time.

Separation between men and women in orthodoxy always bothered me personally, probably due to the fact that since I was a little girl, I always secretly wanted to be a Rabbi. I didn't tell anyone about it until recently, because even I knew how ridiculous

---

[9] Source: Pikiwiki photo stock. Credit: Gal Lalib, 2015.

it sounded in the ears of everyone around me. True, there are women rabbis in Reform Judaism, but that was never 'my thing.' Not yet, anyway. I didn't mind not being a Rabbi, I just wanted to be included.

The heavy presence of the crowd along with the separation always made me feel "unwelcome" or "misplaced." I'm sure I'm not the only one who feels this way. My fondness for history made me travel into fantasies of how the wall used to look before it became the property of the masses.

To my great surprise, my most "Jewish" feeling snuck up on me when I was lost on one of my day tours in the old city. On my way out of the Kotel, I decided to try a new way out and wander around a little bit. I took the northern exit and found myself walking in the main street of the Muslim Quarter. Today, I understand how irresponsible it was of me, but the adventurous sixteen-year-old I was didn't care as much. I asked for directions on how to exit the city and kept walking north, when the area started looking less and less familiar. "Well," I said to myself "I'll just keep walking a little bit further down the street, and if I don't like it, I can always turn back and return to the Western Wall." Little did I know, my feet were carrying me north, along the western platform of the Temple Mount, and were about to bring me to meet a secret Western Wall.

The area around me became more and more "foreign." Women wearing Hijabs and long heavy dresses, tired looking grannies sitting on the floor and selling herbs they picked in the field, mustached men wearing Keffiyehs or religious head coverings, and children running around, either alone or with their parents. The market was filled with smells, a combination of flooding sewage and cooking lamb, freshly baked Pita bread and incense. Hasidic (Ultra-Orthodox Jewish) guys were sticking out in the crowd, walking mostly in pairs, and border police in full uniforms and protective vests followed everyone with their eyes. I started fitting in less and less.

Suddenly, my eyes caught a sign in Hebrew that said "HaKotel HaKatan" - The Small Western Wall, pointing to a side alley. The sign looked beaten. As if it was taken off and put back on several times. 'This is intriguing' I thought, and turned into the alley. The nuance between courage and stupidity can often be lost on a sixteen-year-old. I walked up the alley, ignoring the turns and moving straight ahead. To my surprise, at the end of the alley was a green metal gate, guarded by IDF border police soldiers.

"Hey, how are you guys doing?" I asked and they shrugged. They looked tired. "Do you guys know where the Small Western Wall is?" They pointed me to a side "tunnel" of some sort. It wasn't underground, but it was a dark and semi-long "vault".

"What's in there?" I pointed at the gate they were guarding.

"The Temple Mount," they said.

"Cool!" I responded. "Can I go in?"

"Sorry," the soldier responded. "Only Muslims can enter through here. Are you a Muslim?" he asked with sarcasm, looking at my extremely white skin, my jeans and my tie-dye t-shirt.

"I can be if it helps," I said and salvaged a smile out of him.

Then, I turned into the dark tunnel and found myself in a tiny courtyard, no more than twenty meters long. There it stood, a tiny piece of the Western Wall, completely empty, completely quiet, with no one to set rules, interrupt, or crowd me.

The Small Western Wall, and the vault leading to it, by Oshra Dayan, 2020.

Before taking my first group of tourists to the Wall, I dove deep into its history.

I was born into a Jerusalem that allowed everyone access to the Western Wall, a Jerusalem in which we were safe to pray at the wall, and also a Jerusalem with a giant "Wall area." Little did I know that a large and spacious wall wasn't the experience for most generations of Jews who prayed there.

Historically, the Western Wall stood in close proximity to the residential neighborhoods. A narrow alley alone was made the area for Jews to pray in. To adjust to the new reality, the State of Israel removed an entire neighborhood close to the wall in order to make room for the flood of visitors arriving to the city after 1967 who couldn't pray on the Temple Mount, but were more than grateful to be able to pray at the Western Wall.

Jews praying at the Western Wall, 1898-1914. [10]

The Western Wall Today, 2010[11]

---

[10] Source: Public Domain, 1898-1914.
[11] Source: Pikiwiki photo stock. Credit: Shmulik S. 2010.

This "Little Wall," is actually a twenty-meter segment of the four-hundred-and-eighty-eight-meter-long western platform built by King Herod the Great. Visitors to the wall can easily see the difference between the giant and well chiseled stones, from the time of King Herod, and the later additions made primarily by the Muslims, who renovated the Temple Mount several times throughout history. The structure is so stable it has  lasted a series of massive earthquakes that destroyed many monumental and residential structures in the city. The exceptional stability of it is due to the unique method of construction used by king Herod, called "Dry Build." The construction process didn't require mortar. Nor are there hooks and craters to hold the stones together. The stones stay together in such a smooth and orderly fashion due to impeccable carving and their massive weight. A singular stone from the platform's wall weighs a minimum of a few dozen tons, and usually much more. One of the giant cornerstones weighs five hundred and seventy tons![12]

Traveling in Israel, and particularly in Jerusalem, is taking a trip through history. Repeating the journey our ancestors went through. Even though we weren't there with them, the journey they went through is what made us into who we are today. When the old gets mixed with the new, the core of the experience can get tinted. Here at the Little Wall however, the Western Wall seems just like it looked for centuries.

---

[12] Photo: Muslim stones on top of Herodian stones, Small Western Wall. Source: Pikiwiki photo stock. Credit: Oshrah Dayan, 2020.

The traveling experience through Israel's archeology is different from the travel experience through other monumental locations, like Egypt or Rome. Israel hardly offers anything too impressive to attract people and tempt them to arrive. The best example is a tour guide who thinks that a small courtyard next to some old buildings and a Muslim bathroom stall (we'll get to that), is a worthy enough site to write about in a travel book.

Men and Women Pray together at the Western Wall, 1870.[13]

Israel demands her travelers have vision, the ability to see plenty in what seems like nothing, the ability to dream and experience the world through your imagination. Otherwise, it doesn't have much to give. The traveler to Jerusalem has to believe there is something special about it, and if they do, Jerusalem will give them everything. Otherwise, I've seen travelers who told me that Jerusalem was their least favorite place in the tour and that though they're glad they 'crossed it off their list,' they don't think they will ever return for a second visit.

The visit to the Little Wall is not usually part of the regular tour. It requires intention, and often involves a certain level of personal risk.

---

[13] Source: Public Domain. Credit: Felix Bonfils, 1870.

A visitor to the Little Wall can experience the Western Wall without interruptions and pray in peace. I love going there because I can pray with my friends and my loved ones, with no separation or "excessive and judgmental" eyes. Almost.

True, the Jewish "judgmental eyes," in terms of orthodox religious women or religious rules to narrow my steps in prayer aren't there, but not because they don't want to be there. When this little piece of "Western Wall" was exposed, there were Jewish attempts to "mark it as Jewish," by placing book stands for prayer, chairs, and a library with prayer books, just like you can find at the main Western Wall. The absence of these "territory markers" is due to the fact that the Little Wall is located in the heart of the Muslim quarter. In fact, the northern wall, delimiting the courtyard, is an external wall of a residential home. This may sound strange, but in fact, the western wall of the Temple Mount's platform is not accessible for the most part, as there are many buildings which used it as a "back wall," mainly during the Mamluk and Ottoman periods.

The Small Western Wall and the house built against it, 2020.[14]

---

[14] Source: Pikiwiki photo stock. Credit: Oshrah Dayan, 2020.

Some Muslims who live in the quarter didn't like the Jewish presence attending to the Little Wall, as it is located right in the middle of the Muslim quarter, and next to a "Muslim only" entrance to the Temple Mount. In an attempt to prevent the Jews from arriving at the Little Wall, they built a "bathroom stall" next to it. A urinal of sorts. The "solution" didn't last for long, and the place was sealed and banned from use.

Entrance vault, sealed bathroom stall left to it.
Small Western Wall on the left, Herodian stones at the bottom, 2020.[15]

This however, is a good example of the tiny struggles that make Jerusalem into the mix of religions, feelings and conflicts that it is. About one thousand Jews live inside the Muslim Quarter, all defined by a core belief that Jerusalem must be saved and the

---

[15] Source: Pikiwiki photo stock. Credit: Oshrah Dayan, 2020.

Temple must be built once again. On the Muslim side, core belief is exactly the same, only the other way around.

One day, a construction contractor was sent by the municipality of Jerusalem to strengthen the structures around the wall. Due to his absolute ignorance about the place he was standing at, he decided to drill holes into the Little Western Wall as part of the repair work for the houses around it. Both the Waqf and the Rabbis of Jerusalem were furious. The Rabbi of the Western Wall sadly collected the broken pieces of stone that fell off the wall during the drilling, and buried them in a Jewish cemetery.

Why did the Rabbi decide to give the stones a "proper burial?" Well, this is because of the "bonus" given to those who make the extra effort to see the Little Wall. According to Jewish belief, prayers at the Western Wall tend to "arrive at God's ears" faster, due to the Wall's proximity to the Holy of Holies. Between the two Western Walls, the Little Wall appears to be located closer to the Holy of Holies. It is not for me to have the slightest idea where prayers are being answered at a higher rate, but I'll admit that on top of everything else that is cool about this twenty-meter piece of wall, this is the icing on the cake.

The visit to the Little Wall is life changing. At times, when I find myself needing to ponder, pray, or get in touch with a higher power, I find myself starting my car and driving to the old city, usually at night. Then, I visit the wall while it's empty and the connection to the land and to my ancestors floods me. Along with the "Big Wall" where we can go and pray, I love the fact that Jerusalem hides a "Little Wall" that in so many ways reminds us of the complexity the place holds within it. The gap between what used to be here and what is here now, the conflicts we still have to solve with our neighbors, and the many conflicts we still need to solve among ourselves all make Jerusalem, Jerusalem.

The Western Wall Today, 2019[16]

Jerusalem is deep, and requires such a heavy thought process to comprehend. It is layered and we can study it for decades and never fully understand it. Walking through its allies can be a teachable experience for life. The rebellious teenager in me will forever be grateful to Jerusalem, for due to it I can wholeheartedly say, that cutting school ended up being extremely beneficial to my education.

---

[16] Credit: Seth Stivala, 2019.

PART 4 – THE SOUTH

EIN GEDI SYNAGOGUE

Ein Gedi Synagogue

The lush oasis in Ein Gedi is one of the most visited nature reserves in Israel. Unlike the rest of the sites in this book, it is a part of almost every other itinerary. The gushing waterfalls falling into natural freshwater pools, the rich, dense vegetation and endemic wildlife roaming around - all in the middle of the steaming desert, make this place irresistible and extremely popular.

Most visitors to Ein Gedi walk in the main entrance and disappear into the magic of nature, but not me. Whenever I'm in Ein Gedi without a 'tour rush', I skip the main entrance and walk to the permanent white tent close by. This part of Ein Gedi is hardly toured. There is no running water or impressive vegetation. Underneath the tent, overlooking the dead sea on the east and the Judaean desert's cliff on the west, there is a mosaic floor from a synagogue of a community that lived here more than two thousand, five hundred years ago.

The synagogue itself and its floor are not as old, probably around one thousand, seven hundred years-old, give or take. 'Young' in terms of Jewish history. According to urban legend, or more correctly, desert legend, it was discovered by a Kibbutz member who stumbled upon it during the 1960s, while plowing new fields, revealing the mosaic floors underneath the clods.

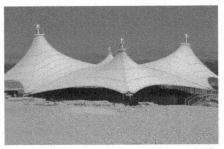

The Tent Shading the Synagogue, 2015[1]

The floor is decorated with geometric patterns. Right in front of the placement for the holy ark[2], in the center of the main hall, is a mosaic of birds. To tell the truth, as far as ancient synagogues go in Israel - I've seen way better. Despite its beauty, this one is far from being the most impressive, nor is it the most well preserved. Most synagogues excavated from the same era have far richer mosaic work, showing characters and even entire scenes from the Torah. Still, the beaten mosaic floor of Ein Gedi is my favorite, not because of what it shows, but because of what it hides.

The Synagogue's Mosaic's Floor, 2015[3]

---

[1] Source: Pikiwiki photo stock. Credit: Shlomi Kakoon, 2015.

[2] In the Holy Ark the Torah scrolls, other holy scriptures and the ritual articles are being stored. As a general rule the holy ark will always be built in the wall of the synagogue that's facing Jerusalem and the Temple. This wall will also be the direction towards which the Jewish community will pray too.

[3] Source: Pikiwiki photo stock. Credit: Shlomi Kakoon, 2015.

Inscriptions in a synagogue's mosaic floor are not a rarity. In our current prayer houses, we will often see plaques thanking donors for their contributions to fund the renovation of a prayer house. In ancient times, these plaques were simply a part of the mosaic floor and the names on it were probably those of the people who paid to have it done. Finding inscriptions like this is common, and the Ein Gedi synagogue is not different and has its fair share of inscriptions on the floor, like the signs of the zodiac, the patriarchs and gratitude to the donors. One inscription however, is unlike any other, and poses a great riddle:

> *"Anyone causing a controversy between a man and his friend / or whoever slanders his friend before the Gentiles or whoever steals / the property of his friend, or* **whoever reveals the secret of the town** */ to the Gentiles—He whose eyes range through the whole earth / and who sees hidden things, He will set his face on that man / and on his seed and will uproot him from under the heavens / And all the people said- Amen and Amen Selah"[4]*

In many synagogues I've seen verses from the Tanakh decorating the interior. Mostly the Ten Commandments, but other verses, too. It is not uncommon for a house of prayer to remind its attendees to follow the rules of The Book, but the rules in this inscription are definitely not from the scriptures. When was the last time your community's house of prayer threatened you to not reveal the town's secret?

"This was no ordinary community", was what I thought the first time I saw it. This inscription is a riddle from the past. A community of Jews was living in this desert, a fair distance from

---

[4] Translation from Hebrew taken from COJS website - Center for Online Jewish Studies.

any settlement big or small, fighting a tough climate with an average temperature of 104°F (40°C), to protect a secret only they knew. Questions started running through my head and I was hooked. What was the secret they were trying to protect? Why did they have to keep it a secret? Did they manage to keep it? And why here of all places?

Segments form the Mosaic's Inscription in Hebrew, 2015[5]

Many scholars have tried to answer these questions, and their suggestions are diverse. One suggested that the secret has something to do with the secrets kept among the Essenes[6].

Qumran is probably the nearest settlement of considerable size to Ein Gedi, a fact that can naturally lead a scholar to believe there would be a continuation of Essenes settlements in the Dead Seat Valley. A similar suggestion is that the guarded secret is some sort of holy scriptures, similar to the Dead Sea Scrolls found near Qumran, that the town was protecting and hiding. An intriguing theory was made by the archeologist Benjamin Mazar, who

---

[5] Source: Pikiwiki photo stock. Credit: Shlomi Kakoon, 2015.
[6] The Essenes were a Second Temple Judaism sect. They followed piety, celibacy and advocated for communal life. On the northern shore of the Dead Sea sits Qumran, a town attributed in research to the Essenes due to, among other things, the discovery of the Dead Sea Scrolls next to it.

suggested that the secret is the community's political stand in the bloody struggle between the Sasanian (Neo-Persian) Empire and the Byzantine Empire.

Under the Byzantine Empire, non-Christian communities were often brutally persecuted. Perhaps the people of Ein Gedi were trying to help the Persians, in an attempt to redeem themselves from the Byzantine burden, and paid the price? This aligns well with the perish of Ein Gedi in the 6th Century AD.

These suggestions are all valid, but none of them, in my humble opinion, takes the cake. My heart goes after the most romantic theory of all, the one that involves love tales between some of the most famous characters in history. Luckily for the hopeless romantic in me, this suggestion is backed up by a lot of research[7].

When ancient Ein Gedi was excavated, vast agricultural infrastructure was revealed in the desert land surrounding it. Irrigated land along with industrial facilities used to process the crops into products. While industrial agriculture doesn't sound very romantic, it also doesn't sound like a big secret. However, these findings are most likely evidence of the most well kept botanical secret in the land of Israel.

Afarsemon Oil: The Rarest Spice of the Highest Price!

In the past, a special oil was produced from a plant that grew exclusively in the Judaean desert. The oil smelled better than any other fragrance in the ancient markets and had qualities beyond count. Many spices were used back then for religious rituals, but none could compare to this one in quality, rarity, or price.

---

[7] Made by scholars Shaul Liberman & Yehuda Felix, and backed by further research brought by Shimshon Ben-Yehusua and Baruch Rozen.

According to the writings of Dioscorides, the Greek physician and botanist, the resin of the plant is a powerful antidote for various poisons and venoms, and that it is very efficient for treating dizziness and epilepsy. Later Jewish doctors of the Middle Ages (their mothers must have been so proud) continue to refer to this ancient plant as a known cure for a long list of illnesses, such as tuberculosis, shortness of breath, indigestion, and dysfunction of internal organs like liver, kidneys, lungs, spleen and even the uterus[8].

The medicinal qualities of this oil should be enough to make it an extremely desired product, but that wasn't all. The Talmud tells us of how the rich daughters of Judaea would 'misuse' the irresistible fragrance of this oil to bring their sinful desires into action. Apparently, those young women would store a few drops of the oil, that was known as a powerful aphrodisiac, in a chicken's crop, and attach it to the heel of their shoe, waiting for desirable men to walk by. When a potential match appeared, they would pop open the crop with their heel, to seduce their "targets" with the intoxicating and enchanting fragrance. How mischievous!

Naturally, the many beneficial qualities of this oil made it very desirable. Alas, the very good things in life seem to always be hard to get. Despite its countless virtues, the oil had one big flaw: The plant only grew in one place in the entire world, in the Judaean desert. In his book 'Natural History', Pliny the Elder documents his findings from his journey to the land of Israel. While accompanying the Roman forces to the land to bring down the

---

[8] Shemesh, A. O. (2013). *Medicinal Plants in Jewish Literature of the Middle Ages and Modern Time: Pharmacology, History, and Halacha.* University of bar Ilan. Ramat Gan. Pp. 256-259.

great rebellion in the First Century AD, Pliny writes that the only land that was 'given' the Afarsemon Oil, was Judaea, and that this plant is superior to all other plants. In fact, it is also said that many merchants tried to disguise their merchandise as Afarsemon oil, and street hawkers would attempt to sell cheap imitations, but the real oil was distinctive and unmistakable[9].

It is curious that despite the plant being described as so superior and so desirable, the only place it grew was a forsaken region in the province of Judaea. How come the growth wasn't expanded to answer the needs of the market? The answer to this question for now, will remain unknown. The reason for that is that the people of Ein Gedi were very successful not only in growing and producing the Afarsemon Oil, but also in their ability to keep a secret. When the community of Ein Gedi perished, all the knowledge regarding the identity of the plant and the process of extracting the oil, perished with them.

This lost knowledge prevents us from knowing the reason the nurturing of this plant was done in this one region and in such small quantities. We can, however, track its fascinating journey throughout history, all the way from the Bible and through some of the best royal love stories in history. Throughout 700 years of honorable and mysterious mentionings in different scriptures and ancient books, not once did the Afarsemon, or the 'Balsam' in its earlier name, ever leave the Judaea desert.

Being lost and unidentified, the Afarsemon Oil was naturally associated with any mysterious fragrant spice or medicinal plant mentioned in local history, some vaguely mentioned, and some that still haven't been identified.

---

[9] Ben-Yosef, S. (2001). *The New Israel Guide*. Volume 13. Judaean Desert and the Dead Sea. Keter Publishing House. Jerusalem. Pp. 208-214

The Queen of Sheba[10]

---

[10] Source: http://breadsite.org .

The first noble love story that could be a lead for the arrival of this mysterious plant to the region is found in the story of King Solomon and the Queen of Sheba. Many tales were told of the exotic queen who formed a unique relationship with the wisest of all men. According to the Biblical story, the Queen of Sheba arrived in King Solomon's kingdom to quiz him and be convinced of his wisdom. After he impresses her with his wits, the Queen bestows him with fabulous gifts. One of those gifts is a unique and rare spice:

> *"Then she gave the king 120 talents of gold, large quantities of spices, and precious stones. There had never been such spices as those the queen of Sheba gave to King Solomon".*

> -   ***2 Chronicles 9:9 NIV***

Whether we choose to read the story and accept it as is, and whether we chose to see it as symbolic of more broad processes that took place at the time, the story of King Solomon and the Queen of Sheba actually aligns quite poetically with current research. The ancient Kingdom of Sheba is thought to be located either in Ethiopia, on the western part of the Red Sea, or in Yemen, on the eastern side of it. These identifications correspond symmetrically with the suggested origins of the Balsam (or Afarsemon), which also are suggested to be Yemen, or Sudan.

Interestingly enough, a unique climate condition to the land of Israel in general and to the Dead Sea Valley in particular is working out quite nicely for this theory. Being the meeting point of three continents (Asia, Europe and Africa), the tiny land of Israel, in its current borders, has in it no less than five different types of climates in it simultaneously: Mediterranean, Saharo-

Arabian, Irano-Turannean, Euro-Sybirian, and Sudanese. The Sudanese climate climbs up the Dead Sea transform fault, right on the seam-line between the tectonic plates of Eurasia and Africa.

This makes the land of Israel the northernmost known habitat of plants that require a Sudanese climate to grow. With the friendly Sudanese habitat of the Dead Sea Valley, the plentiful water from the Ein Gedi oasis and the devoted care of the local Ein Gedi community, the prosperity of a Sudanese plant in Ein Gedi seems quite plausible.

Was the spice given by the Queen of Sheba to King Solomon the Afarsemon? There is no way for us to know. What we do know is that King Solomon is approximated to have lived in around 960 BC, and the earliest findings of settlement we find in Ein Gedi are from 300 years later to that[11].

Nonetheless, the connection between the Afarsemon Oil and great love stories that bring empires together is inevitable. I'm very fond of the story of King Solomon and the Queen of Sheba, mainly because of its amusing current context. Usually, it is the man who brings the woman perfume, and not the other way around, at least according to the old and familiar social construct. This silly little insight makes me admire the Queen of Sheba for her confidence, and her insistence on a lover with a fine aroma.

My contemplations may be a bit silly, but it is common that when a man wants to express affection for a woman he loves, he often gives her perfume. However, what would you do if you were Mark Antony and the woman you loved was Cleopatra? What do you give a woman that already has everything?

---

[11] Ein Gedi had a settlement in it from the Chalcolitic era. The settlement was abandoned due to an unknown reason, and after, the place was resettled in the latter part of the Kingdom of Judaea.

Josephus Flavius, engraving, 1854[12]

Josephus Flavius, a Jew who worked as a historian for the Roman Emperor, documented the history of the Jews in the land of Israel for the Romans. In his writings, we read of a beautiful gesture Mark Antoni made for his beloved Cleopatra, the ruler of Egypt:

> *When Cleopatra had obtained thus much, and had accompanied Antony in his expedition. and passed on to Judea, where Herod met her, and farmed of her parts of Arabia, and those revenues that came to her from the region about Jericho. This country bears that balsam, which is the most precious drug that is there, and grows there alone.*

-   ***The Antiquities of the Jews, Flavius Josephus, Book 15 Chapter 4 Section 1***

It appears that when your beloved is the Queen of Egypt, you don't just give her Balsam oil, you give her the land it grows on and the people who grow it. Mark Antoni was the ruler of Judaea at that

---

[12] Source: Public Domain. Engraving from the book "The Works of Josephus", translation by William Whiston, 1854.

time and King Herod served under his command. In his writings, Josephus describes a terrible rivalry between Cleopatra and Herod. In fact, he goes as far as to say that Herod hated Cleopatra. Nonetheless, the proud queen still lets him run her precious Balsam industry for her, as a servant. We don't know why Cleopatra didn't nominate someone on her behalf to run the business and perhaps even import the secrets to Egypt. Some assume that she may have understood that it would be best to leave such a delicate trade to the people who have the expertise, regardless of her personal feelings. Either way, the secret remained in the hands of the people of Ein Gedi[13].

Cleopatra and Mark Antoni, Lawrence Alma Tadelma 1885. [14]

The Jewish community of Ein Gedi had to have been familiar with foreign attempts to take over their industry. The inscription on the floor of the synagogue is quite clear about the main guidelines: keeping the peace among the community, and not to get in trouble with the Gentiles. Still, one of the worst atrocities done to them in the history of the village, was done to them by their own kin.

---

[13] Ben Yehoshua, S. Rozen, B. (2009). *The Secret of Ein Gedi*. Katedra. Volume 132. Yad Yitzhak Ben Zvi. Jerusalem. Pp. 77-100.

[14] Source: Public Domain. Credit: Lawrence Alma Tadelma 1885.

The people of Ein Gedi had the questionable honor of being a part of the famous and bloody story of Masada, and in the worst way possible.

The story of Masada is one of the most famous in the world. The survivors of the brutal siege escape the attack on Jerusalem and find shelter in Masada, there, in the last remaining stronghold of the great rebellion, they barricaded themselves in a desert fortress. This is the part of the story that got famous. However, a deeper read into the writing of Josephus reveals that before the Temple was destroyed, Masada was already getting "re-populated," and the new arrivals caused nothing but trouble:

> *"And now a fourth misfortune arose, in order to bring our nation to destruction. There was a fortress of very great strength not far from Jerusalem... It was called Masada. Those that were called Sicarii had taken possession of it formerly, but at this time they overran the neighboring countries, aiming only to procure to themselves necessaries; ...they came down by night ...and overran a certain small city called Engaddi:—in which expedition they prevented those citizens that could have stopped them, before they could arm themselves, and fight them. They also dispersed them, and cast them out of the city. As for such as could not run away, being women and children, they slew of them above seven hundred. Afterward, when they had carried every thing out of their houses, and had seized upon all the fruits that were in a flourishing condition, they brought them into Masada".*

> - ***The Wars of the Jews, Flavius Josephus, Book 4, Chapter 7 Sect 2.***

The story of one thousand people committing suicide in Masada became world famous. The seven hundred women and children who were killed in Ein Gedi remained completely anonymous. The zealots rebels, despite being fellow Jews, killed them and stole their possessions and supplies, at least according to Josephus, whose word we should take with a giant boulder of salt.

In the writings of Josephus, we only read about the town of Ein Gedi being robbed and massacred, but we don't get any information about the possession that has been stolen from them.

We mustn't forget who's our source. Josephus was a commander of one of the Jews' rebel forces in the north of the land of Israel. When he is captured by the Romans, he manages to somehow convince them not to kill him, and in an even more miraculous way, becomes the emperor's historian for Jewish matters. Everything Josephus is writing is "infected" with political interests and survival calculations. It is obvious that in the case of Ein Gedi, there is much more that could have been said. Did the people of Ein Gedi manage to keep the secret? Did they die protecting it? Was the valuable stock of Balsam oil taken to Masada?

Part of the information that Josephus hides can be completed by reading the writings of Pliny the Elder. In his documentations of the Romans in the land of Israel, he writes that a great war took place over the Balsam. Apparently, the Jews, 'in their great wickedness,' as written by a Roman historian, were going to burn and destroy the bushes of the Balsam, while the Roman soldiers fought to save them. According to Pliny's description, there was a battle over every single bush!

The defeat of Jerusalem in 70 AD, marked the end of the Great Rebellion. Very few free strongholds of rebels were left after that. Masada was the last.

One thousand men, women and children lived on top of a mountain at the edge of the Empire. To take them down, the emperor sent Plavius Silva at the head of the Roman Legion X Fretensis. The siege was massive and brutal. The rebels didn't stand a chance against the unmatched combat abilities of the Roman army. Josephus points our attention toward the "heroic" act of collective suicide by one thousand people that may or may not have taken place (given that he's the only source, it is hard to cross reference). However, he doesn't answer an important question: Why did the Romans send such a massive force to take down a desert fort with one thousand people, three years after the rebellion had ended?

A fascinating connection between the heavy presence of the Romans in the Judaean Desert, to the Secret of Ein Gedi, is offered by the scholar Zohar Amar[15].

What if Ein Gedi and Masada worked together in cooperation before the Great Rebellion started, and before Masada was taken over by zealots and robbers? What if the fortifications of Masada, along with its massive and well-guarded storage facilities, were also used to store and protect Ein Gedi's precious Balsam oil? That could have provided a strong incentive for the Romans to spend massive resources to take control of Masada. While it appears that, throughout the changing times, the Balsam crops and oil industry couldn't be transferred or copied, it could have been owned. Ownership over the most expensive spice in the empire seems much more valuable than one thousand dead rebels, or one thousand additional slaves.

---

[15] Amar, Z. (2012). *The Afarsemon of Ein Gedi and the Story of Masada.* Studies of Judaea and Samaria. Volume 21. Pp. 227-234

Massive storage facilities in Masada, highly secure, on the berricaded cliff, 2019.[16]

A part of me can't help but wonder about the nature of the relationship between the people of Ein Gedi and the Roman troops. Were the attempts to burn the Balsam bushes done by the people of Ein Gedi, or were these rebels as well? Did the people of Ein Gedi turn to the Romans for help and protection? The Afarsemon Oil was provided locally to Jerusalem and the Temple[17]. With the complete destruction of the local market, did the people of Ein Gedi try to strike a deal with the Romans to help them survive?

---

[16] Credit: Seth Stivala, 2019.

[17] Photo: Incense Altar, from a 17th Century French Map of the Exodus. Source: Public Domain.

250

The Jews of Masada died, but the Jewish community of Ein Gedi continued to exist. Through multiple rebellions and persecutions, the community kept its hold, and probably its trade. The Afarsemon Oil remained a traded good and its price kept rising. During the Byzantine Era, it was said that the price of Balsam oil in Egypt was twice the price of gold!

The ancient synagogue in Ein Gedi was built during the Byzantine era in the land of Israel. At a time of heavy Christian growth and an even heavier persecution of Jews and non-Christian groups, the Judaean desert was filled with monks, lauras and monasteries. The Jews of Ein Gedi lived in a religiously hostile environment, and had to preserve not just their secrets and trades, but their identity as Jews, persecuted in their own homeland, with the absence of a Temple as a center of life.

While synagogues did exist before the destruction of the Temple as some sort of a community center, the concept of synagogues didn't "catch-on" until after the destruction of the Temple. It was then that the synagogue's function expanded from community center to "Mikdash Me'at," a small Temple, a place to keep the practice of Judaism in the absence of the Temple in Jerusalem. This profound understanding of the life of the Jewish community of Ein Gedi at the time in which this synagogue was built, certainly ties the strings together.

Through rebellions and destruction, through massacres and persecution, the community kept on doing what it always did, safeguarding their secret, so they could keep themselves safe. Under these conditions, it is no wonder the rules of the community found their way into the synagogue, which became the living heart of a Jewish community without a Temple.

In the 6th Century AD, something happened to the people of Ein Gedi.

The ancient settlement didn't give away many signs to indicate the reason for their disappearance. Some guess they died under the brutal hand of the Byzantine Emperor, Justinian I in his persecutions of non-Christian groups. Some say it was a plague.

Whatever had happened, the Arab conquest of 638 AD followed, which started the Early Muslim period in the land, and ended the trade of Balsam Oil. The community of Ein Gedi was gone, along with their unique knowledge and any traces of the delicate crop. Repeated research attempts were made for centuries to try and identify the real Afarsemon. Many suggestions were made, but none have hit the bullseye, so far. The Afarsemon's identification is still a mystery today.

After centuries of survival, the community of Ein Gedi didn't live to tell the tale. On the other hand, the people of Ein Gedi always excelled in keeping their secrets.

Panoramic View of Ein Gedi and the Dead Sea, 2013.[18]

I think this is why, when everyone else is running to the cool freshwater pools, I come here again and again to look at the mosaic inscription in the synagogue. An entire community gone,

---

[18] Source: Pikiwiki photo stock. Credit: Shirley Saramito, 2013.

leaving us no information about it, except for one detail: They had a secret. And if they did their job right, that's perhaps all that we are ever going to know. A secret is an element so inclusive, yet excluding at the same time. With their secret or without it, this community suffered the same end as the rest of the Jewish communities in the land. It is perhaps for this reason, that even without knowing, I like to stand alone for a few moments in their synagogue, and share their silence with them.

SECRET ISRAEL

MOUNT TZFAHOT

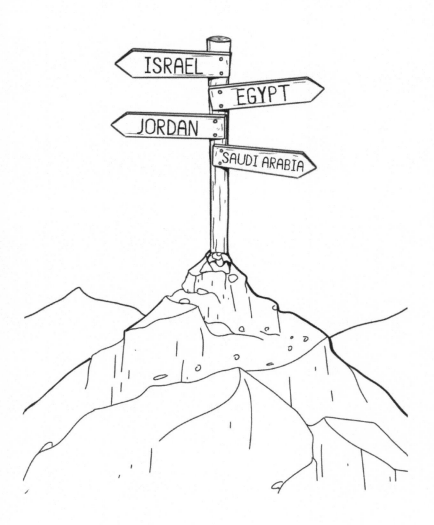

Mount Tzfahot

Most places in Israel are rich with human remains and information. They are often thousands of years old, and have a crucial role in helping us understand our development as a human society, thus developing a better understanding of ourselves in the present. Sometimes however, in order to think and see with clarity, we can't look at all of the human remains, at "junk", figuratively speaking, we see laying around everywhere. Sometimes a person has to leave home, and climb to a bare mountain top in a barren country, just to get the thoughts in order. Mount Tzfahot is the perfect location to start or end a journey. It is a scenic point of clarity, and it is a perfect place to take in the spiritual meaning of Israel.

One of my most memorable moments on Mount Tzfahot was when I climbed it alone. The day before a tour, I climbed to the top so I could see it. Two-hundred, seventy-eight meters of climbing stood between me and the floating wonder. I arrived at the top, looked toward the Red Sea and finally, there she was. The aircraft carrier of the US military. I could see all of it from up here. Earlier that day I drove five hours from my house in Tel Aviv to Eilat, and arrived in the afternoon. I had just enough time before the sun set, and decided to climb the mountain, to catch a full view of this monster, before meeting the people who live in it.

I felt the excitement building up inside of me as I witnessed the magnitude of this vessel, just floating in the water. The next day I was going to meet a group of American soldiers from the aircraft carrier, and take them on a day tour in Jerusalem. It wasn't just me, of course. I worked for a tour agency back then, and it was a whole operation. We had a small fleet of buses, to fit all of the residents of this floating town.

Witnessing the presence of the US military always has an impact on me. The size, the capacity, the efficiency. All were bigger than anything I knew. The IDF[1] was my military, and reputation aside, on a personal level everything always felt so…small, even cozy. Perhaps it's the fact that our military service is mandatory, which makes the military an integral part of our lives, and thus, less exhilarating. Maybe it's just because in Israel everything has to be smaller, we barely all fit here as it is. Either way, I was excited and really looking forward to the encounter with the American soldiers.

Whenever I meet American soldiers or veterans, we almost always manage to create a feeling of closeness, of mutual understanding. Not just because we both served in the military, but I believe it is mainly because they've been around here, in the Middle East, and they understand a fragment of the crazy reality we live in.

I stood on top of the mountain and felt the breeze going through my hair and drying my face, that was sweaty and probably red from the climb. I felt the hard and exposed schist rock through my shoes and took in the rough terrain of the red and naked desert mountains of Eilat.

I didn't pick this mountain top randomly. Mount Tzfahot is probably the best lookout point in the whole Eilat area. It isn't

---

[1]Israeli Military's abbreviation, standing for Israeli Defense Force

necessarily the highest or the most beautiful, but it is by far the most symbolic spot of them all. For starters, it is probably one of the most ancient mountain tops in Israel. The mountains of Eilat, in general, are among the oldest rocks in the land, but Mount Tzfahot is a good ol' Grandpa Mountain, celebrating the proud age of eight hundred and thirty million years-old (maybe that's why he's bold). This mountain might be old, but one of its best qualities is that it always stays up to date with the latest news. When standing on top of this mountain, you can gaze at four states, all at once: Egypt, Jordan, Saudi Arabia and Israel. That's not a sight you forget.

Panoramic View of the Red Sea, 2013.[2]

---

[2] Credit: Jed Fluxman, 2013.

Straight South from me is the Eilat Bay and the beach of the Red Sea, and there was the carrier silently floating in it. The proportions seemed almost as if someone had built a city made of legos and placed it to float in the tub. It looked so small from where I stood, yet I couldn't help but think of all of the big things it must have done, and all of the big topics I wanted to talk about with the US military folks. Our itinerary was already set in stone and Jerusalem-bound, but I knew right there and then that if I'd had it my way, I'd have shown them all the view from the mountaintop. We would leave early in the morning, when it was still dark outside. Then we'd climb the mountain together and watch the sun rising over Jordan. We would gaze southeast, to see it sending a soft light towards the coast of Saudi Arabia, and regret we couldn't stay to see it set over Egypt that evening.

Sunset View from Mt. Tzfahot, 2015.[3]

Our Geopolitical Neighborhood - Island Fever's Cause #1

This place always reminds me of why me, and so many Israelis like me, get island fever so often. To many people, Israel seems

---

[3] Credit: Inbal Elisheva Arazi Berman, 2015.

like the colonial superpower of the Middle East. Even those of us who are perfectly aware of its size, we all still get that small familiar 'mini-shock' when we look at the map of the Middle East for the one thousand time and remember again just how small we really are. The entire country is eight thousand, five hundred and fifty square miles, almost twenty-three thousand square kilometers, and unlike New Jersey, which is equal to Israel in size, our neighbors are not Pennsylvania or Canada. No matter where you drive to, the road is going to end in less than a day, because there is no crossing the border.

Our neighboring countries, north and clockwise, are Lebanon, Syria (who's currently hosting Iran on our border, time will tell how this will end), Jordan and Egypt. Saudi Arabia is close enough to see and wave "hello" to from the Eilat Bay, but we don't in fact share a border, though technically it is possible to walk from Israel to the Saudi border in a day.

In Israel we have a population of nine million on just eight thousand, five hundred square miles. For the sake of comparison, the Kingdom of Jordan is thirty-four thousand square miles with a population of ten million, Egypt is three hundred and ninety thousand square miles with a population of one hundred million, and Saudi Arabia is eight hundred and thirty thousand square miles with approximately thirty-four million people living there[4]. All of the states around this bay are Suni Muslim, as opposed to Lebanon and Syria that border us from the north, which are both currently Shiite ruled. Given that the real war in the Middle East is between the Shiite and the Sunni, Israel found itself a good seat, right in the middle.

When I stand here and look down, the pointy edge of Eilat's coast in the Red Sea makes Israel look like a shim, wedged in and snug,

---

[4] All data (2019).

somehow separating the polarized forces of the Middle East. It is a helluva neighborhood to live in. The Muslim world and countries work with different codes, ethics and orientation than the western world. As a private citizen, the Israeli distance and isolation from the western family of nations is often smothering. Brutally disregarding Israel's domestic issues, which are plenty, complex, and often bear an explosive potential, our near neighbors are very different, and the feeling can get quite lonely.

Personally, I believe that this is one of the main reasons for the phenomenon of "Island Fever" among Israelis. Incomes in Israel are far from being the highest in the western world and our cost of living is very high. Still, Israelis are known to travel internationally more than any other population. Just to wet the whistle, in the year 2018, Israel had a population of eight million, eight hundred thousand, and in that year, there were eight million, four hundred thousand departures of Israeli citizens traveling abroad[5]. Island fever didn't skip me over either. As much as I love Israel, and I do with all my heart, I often find myself making international traveling a financial priority, and I'm not alone. Maybe it's our way of taking a vacation from being so… snug in our complex little neighborhood.

It's Not Easy Being Green

"It's not easy being green…" Sir Kermit the Frog sang and I deeply identify. As Israeli Jews, we carry a "package" when we travel the world, and I believe one of its key elements lies in the unique situation of our "natural habitat."

On one hand, we live the life of a western society. Israel is a democracy, our citizens have equal rights and human rights, and

---

[5] Israel's Tourism Report 2018, **Central Bureau of Statistics.**

our government's system of checks and balances works, which we know because neither side of the political aisle is happy about it. Many of us watch American television and almost everyone can communicate in basic English that's being taught in schools.

On the other hand, things aren't that simple. For starters, we are not Europe, the US or Canada. We are a western country in the beating, or perhaps racing, heart of the Middle East. Our circumstances are very different and we carry a very different life experience. It starts with the most basic things, for instance, the elementary sense of security.

The reality of living in Israel is that each and every one of us, no matter where we live or our affiliations, experience war, in one way or the other. There is no escaping it. Mandatory military service aside, though granted it is a significant influence as well, there is no place in Israel that's too far from the border, from areas of conflict or that's out of the missile range of Hezbollah in the north, or Hamas in the south. The reality is that in Israel, you can't be ten years-old, and not remember the last war.

One of the consequences of this reality is that despite being a part of "western society," we don't share the feeling of "Pax Romana," of relative regional stability that promises a sense of personal security that other people in the rest of the Western World have. Growing up in the shadows of war and vivid existential threats forms a different life experience, and often forms a different view of the world.

Conversations with people from the western world then tend to hit a wall more often than not. It is hard to understand an existential threat when you never experience it, so in conversations over the situation in Israel, which is starring in the news like it's the seasonal ball games, I often feel that one side speaks of ideals, notions and theories, while the other side speaks about reality and real-life experience from the ground. Agreement is rarely found.

The first time I experienced it was when I went to a dance festival in a country in Western Europe. It was an international festival and there were dancers from all over the world, which mainly meant Europe and the US. There aren't many swing dancers in the Middle East or Africa nowadays. It was summer, and I was excited to take a vacation and go swing dancing abroad, for the first time in my life.

My excitement faded quickly when two days after my arrival, war broke out in Israel. It was 2014, one of our hardest and bloodiest operations in Gaza. Missiles were flying and landing on residential buildings in my hometown, targeting families. My best friend was called to his reserve unit and sent into Gaza. So was my brother. So were many of my close friends. Two years before, I was working at a pre-military training program, and many of my students were soldiers at that time. Many of them were sent into Gaza as well. I was worried and felt sick to my stomach, but everyone around me was dancing, and that's what I came to do.

I remember tearing myself away from the news, trying not to check more often than twice a day, so I could enjoy the festival. I asked a friend who had some clearance in the IDF to send me the list of soldiers who died every day, just so I'd know if any of my friends or former students were among the names. And everyone around was dancing. It was surreal.

With this very awkward feeling, I was still on my vacation and everyone at home encouraged me to enjoy myself as much as I could. My surprise, I remember, came from a completely unexpected direction. Swing dance festivals are probably one of the most social events out there, simply because you cannot enjoy your time without interacting with other people and asking them to dance. It is the whole point of the entire event. In this setting, I experienced for the first time what "being green" meant.

Since Israel makes it to world news whenever anything like that happens, people in the festival were very much aware of the situation. Many of my social interactions from that point on were awkward and uncomfortable, if I were lucky. I'd often introduce myself, and as soon as I said I was from Israel, people would find some sort of excuse to leave the conversation and go someplace else. In worse scenarios, I found myself being verbally "attacked" and cornered into political arguments, where I was "explained to" that fewer Jews died so far, and that's just isn't fair. This, and other pearls of wisdom that are simply too shameful to even waste paper and ink on. Political arguments are the least of my concern and I believe whole-heartedly that they're vital to our existence as a healthy society. What bothered me most of all were the many reactions that varied on a range between revulsion and a complete lack of empathy. The uncompromising refusal to acknowledge the complexity of the situation or sympathize with my personal experience, became a memory that had a tremendous influence on shaping my identity.

Mount Tzfahot symbolizes for me a place where the complexity of Israel displays itself in a glorious manner. Understanding the implications of being an independent Jewish state in a Muslim neighborhood is a hard thing to do. It is the living experience that shapes your personality more than anything else. I believe that a visit to Mount Tzfahot can provide life experience and grant a profound understanding of life in this crazy land.

The God Element

Most of the popular sites in Israel are in the central or northern part of the country. It is understood. Most of the population is there too, and when it comes to both ancient and modern cultures, it's obvious that most of them would find it more suitable to live in a land of water and vegetation.

Nonetheless, there is a core ingredient in the existence of our nation, that comes from the desert, and it had an impact not just on our lives, but on our historical development as a monotheistic-oriented worldly society. Whether we like it or not, modernity, enlightenment and secularism as social phenomena are a product of recent centuries, they didn't pop out of thin air. We live today in what is commonly called Judeo-Christian society, due to the fact that our values, morals and foundational thinking is based on the Bible.

History teaches us that paganism is a natural tendency in human nature, given that historic societies around the world were, by and large, paganistic. In the land of Israel though, something happened that influenced the world. That special something had to do a lot with the desert.

Biblical stories aside, archeological anthropology teaches us that when we examine ancient cultures, the deities of the desert are very different in their physical manifestations than the deities of the "settled" land. In the settled land, where water and vegetation can be found, the shapes of the idols are more expressive. They have noses and eyes and ears, and there are many of them. One for rain, one for trees, one for fertility, one for war, etc.

In a land of plenty, there is more than enough to go around. This is reflected in the idols of these regions. However, the story of desert nations is very different. Nations who dwelled in the desert were often either half or fully nomadic[6]. A single visit to the desert

---

[6] Half-nomadic refers to a tribe moving in rotation between a number of territories according to the seasons of the weather.

is enough to make anyone understand how hard life can be, and how a simple thing like having water to drink can become an existential threat. The deities found in ancient desert societies were different. The idols weren't figures, but hewn stones, representing the center of prayer and perhaps a spiritual intention toward a higher power.

In light of these observations about ancient deities, the formation of monotheism in the desert by a nomadic tribe collectively experiencing a revelation of God, makes sense. The revolutionary impact of this concept is not in its formation, but by its spread from its reign in the desert to the settled land.

The location of the land of Israel, as I've mentioned before, is unique in so many ways that simultaneously cause and complement each other. In Israel is the northernmost appearance of the desert climate in the world (the Judaean Desert). Inside the land, between the line of Beer-Sheva, Hebron and Jerusalem, is the link between the desert and the settled land. That is where the two different deities met, fought, and clashed. The story of the Israelites conquering the promised land is in many ways the story of a desert nation with a desert deity, penetrating the settled realm and changing its ways of thinking and ways of life down to the core.

Standing at the top of Mount Tzfahot often makes me think of the revelation of God before the nation of Israel at Mount Sinai. On a personal level, I feel like it makes perfect sense. A nation of people of the desert with nothing around them but rocks and mountains. Nothing in the desert except for them and the higher power that's guiding them and providing for them. It seems that belief in a higher power, whether we possess it or not, must come from nothing. It must come from that empty, desolate and abandoned place inside of us that searches for meaning, guidance and supervision.

Moses on Mount Sinai, Gérôme Jean-Léon 1895[7]

There is no better representation for such emptiness than the rocky, barren and ancient rocks of Mount Tzfahot. The landscape offers nothing but bare, ancient mountains as far as the eye can see. The mountains themselves are so old, they reflect nothing but Godly power. The search to connect with a power so great and absolute and the desire to unite with it is in our nature, and on top of this mountain, it is very hard to ignore.

Ascending Mt. Tzfahot, 2013[8]

---

[7] Source: Public Domain. Credit: Gérôme Jean-Léon -1895-1900.
[8] Credit: Jed Fluxman, 2013

The Wondering Jew

The association with Mount Sinai often makes me think of our presence as Jews in the land of Israel today.

The existence of the State of Israel as a Jewish state among the nations of the world is heavier and more complex than a book chapter can even begin to unwrap. Still, life as a Jew in Israel often reveals the magnitude of challenges, and the importance of staying strong in the face of them.

On a domestic level, there are difficulties beyond count in being a Jewish nation. I have yet to meet two Jews who agreed with each other on more than one topic. We may be merely 0.2% of the world's population, but we are as different as it comes. There are core ideas that bind us together, like the need for survival. This need is way beyond the survival of an ethnic or religious group. It is the need to survive as the bearers of a historical torch that changed the world.

In the development of monotheistic civilizations across the world, Christianity and Islam clashed more than once. Christianity stemmed from Judaism, and bound its New Testament with the Old. Islam leaned on both Judaism and Christianity and developed a path of its own. The land of Israel is the historical heart of this confrontation, and more than a thousand years later, the conflict is still boiling around us.

The attempt to sustain a Western Jewish nation in this exact spot often strikes me with how insane it seems as a notion, yet how natural it feels when you live it.

I couldn't see myself living anywhere else, nor with any other identity than this.

Far be it from me to determine the existence or intentions of a higher power. The only thing I know is that as a Jew in the land and country of Israel, I see meaning in every act and every choice. How we live our lives in general has a tremendous impact on our environment, and when our environment is a Jewish country in the heart of the conflicted Middle East, the meaning becomes crucial to existence.

Looking down from Mount Tzfahot on the American Aircraft carrier made me realize something important. While our societies are not ruled by religion, Judeo-Christian culture as a wholesome concept is one of the main shapers of our identity, values, and morals. When I look at the challenges our world is facing today, the violence, the greed and the fanaticism, I am struck by how much work needs to be done. Not to achieve a utopia. I've never believed in utopias. As a matter of fact, I believe that the unattainable nature of utopias is often the root of all evil. I am struck by how much work needs to be done just to achieve a decent state of survival, and a pleasant life of coexistence.

Maybe this is why I get along so well with American soldiers and veterans. Throughout my career as a guide, I've met many different people from many different countries, and heard countless points of view and opinions about the world. After all that I've experienced, I often feel that Israel and America, this is of course a huge generalization, share a similar understanding of the atrocities this world is filled with, and the challenges we are all facing. We don't even have to agree on the best way to solve them, but I do believe that this joint understanding might be the foundation of the strong partnership between Israel and the United States.

The sun started setting and it was time to leave my beloved mountain top and go prepare my guiding sessions for the next day.

Before I left, I gave it all one last look. The American aircraft carrier snuggled in the little bay by three Muslim countries, and anchored in the tiny Eilat Bay in Israel. Tomorrow I was going to take a bus filled with American soldiers from the desert to Jerusalem, the capital and beating heart of Israel. I got excited when I thought of all the things I would show them as we drive through the desert towards the "settled land." The farms, the biotechnological developments, the cities and the universities, and even the relative peace we managed to create with our neighbors, Egypt and Jordan. It all made me proud. Despite all of the complexities, the challenges and conflicts, we've built something beautiful here.

We've built something strong and improving and self-checking and even free, to some extent. We've built a country that I am proud to speak for and proud to stand behind, knowing very well what it represents in this world.

The words of our first prime minister popped into my head:

"In the desert the country of Israel will be tested."

- ***David Ben-Gurion***

Boy, was he right. This land is where we came from and where we became who we are. It is up to us to make it into a place that is worthwhile to exist in this world. With all the difficulties that it brings, above all, physically and spiritually, this is home. It is on us to make it into a home we are proud of.

Finally, it was time to climb down from the mountain and go do the two things I love the most: Talk about Israel, and make new friends.

About the Author

Shakked Beery – The Wandering Jewess
Author, Speaker, Tour Guide.

Native to the land for ten generations, Shakked and Israel are one. After finishing her service in the IDF, she decided to combine her love for the land with her talent for storytelling, and became a full-time tour guide and speaker. The profession soon became a life mission, to serve as a connecting link between visitors and Israel. Shakked is a certified tour guide by the Israeli Ministry of Tourism, and a lecturer in the Israeli School of Tourism. Her credentials are based on a Master's degree in Israel Studies from the University of Haifa, and countless hours of passionate independent research about anything and everything she finds interesting. Nowadays, Shakked divides her time between Israel and the US, guiding tours or speaking to audiences, telling stories about the Israel she loves.

Shakked's Website:
wanderingjewess.com

Contact Shakked:
wjewess@gmail.com

Acknowledgements

To **Seth Stivala** (The Outsider), for being my writing role-model and my partner in crime, for pulling my writing-wagon out of the mud, and for always believing in me, whether I'm down in the gutters or on top of the world. It is only because of you that I had the courage to make this happen. Thank you, Cowboy.

To **Dillon Krueger** (from Real Patriot Publishing), for the heart-stirring illustrations, heart-to-heart conversations, a unique friendship, and for being part of the inspiration for writing this book.

To **Bonnie & Reg Nekl** (from Reg's 7 Mile Steakhouse, where the best steaks hide from the rest of the world), who didn't owe me anything and gave me everything. For putting a roof over my head, and steaks in my belly. Thank you, Bonnie, my Nebraska Mama and friend, for your incredible hospitality, and thank you for believing in me and helping me make my dreams a reality.

To **Ganit Aliad**, who is my guiding light and mentor, who brought me out of great darkness and loss into capability and light. This book, like many other good things in my life, would never have happened without you. Thank you for the unique presence that you are in this world.

To **Dr. Nurit Shtober-Zisu**, Head of the Israel Studies Department at Haifa University in Israel, who made me realize that geology is not as terrible as math (and that's as far as I'll go). Who gave me the right push at the right time, for helping me with the chapters about Ateret (Chastellet) and Mount Schists, and for always having the best interests of her students and her country at heart.

To **Dr. Shimon Gat**, my mentor and inspiration for guiding, for his contribution to the chapter about Ramla, and for his contribution to my guiding career and smiles in general.

To **Yaron Ben-Ami**, the most mind-blowing teacher and speaker out there, who got me hooked on the antiquities of my people, and made me realize that the Jewish story just might be more badass than rock 'n' roll. Thank you for endless inspiration and advice over the years my good friend. Counting on you to always stay chayav.

To my sister, **Or Beery**, a first-class photographer and visualist, for contributing to the writing process in general, and more specifically for the chapter about the Cistern of Arches, with original ideas and wit, and for her observant consultancy about the cover design. Thanks sis.

To **Sam Sacks** who came to the rescue and did a helluva job editing this book.

To my dear friends, **Jed Fluxman, Inbal Elisheva Arazi, Nora Buller, and Janet Kaplan**, who came to the rescue and contributed their fabulous photographs for the chapter about Mount Tzfahot. Thank you for your generosity, and for your friendship.

To **George Rath**, who listened intently to chapters of this book as it was written, and provided wise advice. For enduring tears, complaints, and bad jokes throughout the entire process. For being my partner for deep conversations about lofty ideas and long philosophical discussions. For patiently listening to my long-winded concepts, and for always offering support and brainstorming whenever it was needed. Thank you, my good friend.

To my mother, **Elana Beery**, who values education above all, for always providing a safety net and means for progress for my crazy ideas. Who helped format the book for publishing, and encouraged me throughout the entire process. Thank you for supporting me throughout my often unorthodox decisions, and for being proud of me and allowing me to find my own path.

To my best friend **Nitzan Begger**, for being the best friend a girl could ask for. For never missing a chance to be there when times get hard, and for always pumping into my brain that things are going to be great, no matter how harsh reality may seem.

To the rest of my friends, family, and everyone I did not mention. I am blessed. My life is filled with good people and support, and I am grateful for each and every one of you.

SECRET ISRAEL

Bibliography

Amar, Z. (2012). *The Afarsemon of Ein Gedi and the Story of Masada*. Studies of Judaea and Samaria. Volume 21. Pp. 227-234

Amit, H. Amit, D. (2005). *Marei Makom, Reference Points. Traveling with the Jewish Sources in Northern Israel*. Yad Yizhak Ben Zvi. Jerusalem. Pp. 76-87

Ankori, M. (2020). *Rujum El Hiri - The Riddle of Unity*. Online Lecture.

Anonymous. (1975). *At Dawn - Diary Chapters*. Translation of Alexander Zaid's diary from Russian to Hebrew. Original Publisher: Am Oved. Electronic Version: Ben-Yehuda Project.

Avni, G. (2011). *Continuity and change in the cities of Palestine during the Early Islamic period.*

Barkai, G. (2016). *Yad Absalom - The Tomb of Herod Agripa King of Judah*. Researches of The City of David. Jerusalem.

Ben Yehoshua, S. Rozen, B. (2009). *The Secret of Ein Gedi*. Katedra. Volume 132. Yad Yitzhak Ben Zvi. Jerusalem. Pp. 77-100

Ben-Yosef, S. (2001). *The New Israel Guide*. Volume 13. Judaean Desert and the Dead Sea. Keter Publishing House. Jerusalem. Pp. 208-214

Boas, A. (1999). *Crusader archaeology: the material culture of the Latin East*. Routledge. Pp. 115

Bolton, A. T., ed. (1925). *"St Paul's Cathedral"*. The Wren Society. Oxford University Press. Pp: 15–20.

Breslavi, Y. (1964). *Jerusalem's Guide from the Cairo Geniza*. The Company for the Research of the Land of Israel and its Antiquities, Israel.

Eish Shalom, M. (1965). *Christian Pilgrimages to the Land of Israel*. Am-Oved & Dvir. Tel-Aviv. Pp. 249-250.

Ellenblum, R. Marco, S. Agnon, A. Rockwell, T. Boas, A. (1998). *Crusaders Castle Torn Apart by Earthquake at Dawn*, 20 May 1202. Hebrew University. Jerusalem. Pp. 1-4.

Gat, S. (n.d.). *The Story of Ramla, the City that Wandered*. Ramle Municipality's Official Website.

Gat, S. (n.d.). *Many Cisterns and One Aqueduct - The Water Supply to Ancient Ramla*.

Gabai M. Yitzhaki, G. (2001). *The New Israel Guide*. Volume 4. Keter. Yediot Ahronot. Israeli Ministry of Defense. Jerusalem. Pp. 57-65.

Goren, Y. (n.d.). *The Jerusalem Syndrome in Biblical Archeology*. Forum Archives. Society of Biblical Literature.

Hebrew University of Jerusalem. (2007). *Vadum Iacob Research Project. The Templar Castle of Vadum Iacob - "Jacob's Ford"*. Official Website.

Israel's Tourism Report 2018, Central Bureau of Statistics.

Kamar, A. (2016). *Gilgal Rephaim - The Mysterious Site in the Golan Heights*. Ecology & Science. Ynet.

Karpel, D. (2003). *One Day, The Letters Came Out*. Ha'aretz.

L. Dindrof. I, Bonn. (1832). *Chronicon Paschale*, ed. (p. 474)

Marcus, M. (2001). *The New Israel Guide*. Volume 2. Hermon, Golan, and the Hula Valley. Keter Publishing House. Jerusalem. Pp. 104-105.

Mendelboim S. (2014). *The Figure and Actions of Avraham Shlomo Zalman Tzoref - HaRashaz*. Beit Solomon - Three Generations to the Founder of the Yeshuv. Zalman Shazar. Jerusalem. Pp. 25.

Morgenstern, A. (2006). *Hastening Redemption: Messianism and Resettlement of the Land of Israel*. Oxford University Press. Pp. 11.

Morgenstern, A. (2007). *The Return to Jerusalem: The Jewish Resettlement of Israel, 1800-1860*, Shalem Center, Jerusalem. Pp. 3.

Municipality of Jerusalem. (2017). *Neighborhoods in Jerusalem*. The Official Website of the Municipality of Jerusalem.

Parkash, T. Mendelbaum, E. (2016). *Not Just the Western Wall - The Forgotten and Holier Wall*. Ynet Judaism. Ynet

Regev, Y. (2001). *The New Israel Guide*. Volume 6. Yediot Ahronot. Israeli Ministry of Defense. Keter. Jerusalem. Pp. 119-121.

Safrai, Z. (2001). *The History and Importance of Beit Shearim*. Gatherings of the Land of Israel. Ariel 147-148. Jerusalem. Pp. 11-25.

Schremer, A. (1987). *More About Uzziah's Tomb*. Katedra Periodical. Yad Yizhak Ben Zvi, Jerusalem.

Shemesh, A. O. (2013). *Medicinal Plants in Jewish Literature of the Middle Ages and Modern Time: Pharmacology, History, and Halacha*. University of bar Ilan. Ramat Gan. Pp. 256-259.

Twain, M. (1899) *Concerning the Jews*. Harper's Magazine.

All Rights Reserved to